THE ROMAN RITUAL

REVISED BY DECREE OF THE
SECOND VATICAN ECUMENICAL COUNCIL
AND PUBLISHED
BY AUTHORITY OF POPE PAUL VI

THE
RITE OF PENANCE

APPROVED FOR USE
IN THE
DIOCESES OF THE UNITED STATES OF AMERICA
BY THE NATIONAL CONFERENCE
OF CATHOLIC BISHOPS
AND
CONFIRMED BY THE APOSTOLIC SEE

ENGLISH TRANSLATION
PREPARED
BY THE INTERNATIONAL COMMISSION
ON ENGLISH IN THE LITURGY

PUEBLO PUBLISHING COMPANY

NEW YORK

Concordat Cum Originali:
+ James P. Mahoney, D. D.
Vicar General, Archdiocese of New York

Published by authority of the Bishops' Committee on the Liturgy,
National Conference of Catholic Bishops.

Design: Frank Kacmarcik, D.F.A.

English translation of The Rite of Penance. Copyright ©
1974, International Committee on English in the Liturgy, Inc.
All rights reserved.

The text of the Bible included in this ritual is taken from The
Jerusalem Bible and used by permission of Doubleday & Company, Inc.
Copyright © 1966 by Darton, Longman & Todd, Ltd. and Doubleday & Company,
Inc.

The text of the Psalms included in this ritual is taken from the Grail Psalter
© The Grail (England) 1963. The Complete Grail Psalms were first published in 1963
by—and are available through—William Collins Sons & Co. Limited
except in North America where they are available through
the Paulist Press Inc. and Collins and World Publishing Company.

English translation of the Magnificat by the
International Consultation on English Texts.

Printed in the United States of America

CONTENTS

THE
RITE OF PENANCE

SACRED CONGREGATION FOR DIVINE WORSHIP

Prot. n. 800/73

DECREE

Reconciliation between God and men was brought about by our Lord Jesus Christ in the mystery of his death and resurrection (see Romans 5:10). The Lord entrusted the ministry of reconciliation to the Church in the person of the apostles (see 2 Corinthians 5:18ff). The Church carries this ministry out by bringing the good news of salvation to men and by baptizing them in water and the Holy Spirit (see Matthew 28:19).

Because of human weakness, Christians "turn aside from [their] early love" (see Revelation 2:4) and even break off their friendship with God by sinning. The Lord, therefore, instituted a special sacrament of penance for the pardon of sins committed after baptism (see John 20:21-23), and the Church has faithfully celebrated the sacrament throughout the centuries—in varying ways, but retaining its essential elements.

The Second Vatican Council decreed that "the rite of formulas of penance are to be revised in such a way that they may more clearly express the nature and effects of this sacrament."[1] In view of this the Congregation for Divine Worship has carefully prepared the new *Rite of Penance* so that the celebration of the sacrament may be more fully understood by the faithful.

In this new rite, besides the *Rite for Reconciliation of Individual Penitents*, a *Rite for Reconciliation of Several Penitents* has been drawn up to emphasize the relation of the sacrament to the community. This rite places individual confession and absolution in the context of a celebration of the word of God. Furthermore, for special occasions a *Rite for Reconciliation of Several Penitents with General Confession and Absolution* has been composed in accordance with the Pastoral Norms on

[1] Second Vatican Council, constitution *Sacrosanctum Concilium*, no. 72: *AAS* 56 (1964) 118.

General Sacramental Absolution, issued by the Congregation for the Doctrine of the Faith on June 16, 1972.[2]

The Church is solicitous in calling the faithful to continual conversion and renewal. It desires that the baptized who have sinned should acknowledge their sins against God and their neighbor and have heartfelt repentance for them, and it tries to prepare them to celebrate the sacrament of penance. For this reason the Church urges the faithful to attend penitential celebrations from time to time. This Congregation has therefore made regulations for such celebrations and has proposed examples or specimens which episcopal conferences may adapt to the needs of their own regions.

Accordingly Pope Paul VI has by his authority approved the *Rite of Penance* prepared by the Congregation for Divine Worship and ordered it to be published. It is to replace the pertinent sections of the *Roman Ritual* now in use. The rite in its Latin original is to come into force as soon as it is published, but vernacular versions will be effective from the day determined by the episcopal conferences, after they have approved the translation and received confirmation from the Apostolic See.

Anything to the contrary notwithstanding.

From the office of the Congregation for Divine Worship, December 2, 1973, the First Sunday of Advent.

By special mandate of the Pope

Jean Cardinal Villot
Secretary of State

✝ Annibale Bugnini
Titular Archbishop of Diocletiana
Secretary of the Congregation for Divine Worship

[2]See *AAS* 64 (1972) 510-514.

INTRODUCTION

I

THE MYSTERY OF RECONCILIATION IN THE HISTORY OF SALVATION

1. The Father has shown forth his mercy by reconciling the world to himself in Christ and by making peace for all things on earth and in heaven by the blood of Christ on the cross.[1] The Son of God made man lived among men in order to free them from the slavery of sin[2] and to call them out of darkness into his wonderful light.[3] He therefore began his work on earth by preaching repentance and saying: "Turn away from sin and believe the good news" (Mark 1:15). This invitation to repentance, which had often been sounded by the prophets, prepared the hearts of men for the coming of the Kingdom of God through the voice of John the Baptist who came "preaching a baptism of repentance for the forgiveness of sins" (Mark 1:4).

Jesus, however, not only exhorted men to repentance so that they should abandon their sins and turn wholeheartedly to the Lord,[4] but he also welcomed sinners and reconciled them with the Father.[5] Moreover, by healing the sick he signified his power to forgive sin.[6] Finally, he himself died for our sins and rose again for our justification.[7] Therefore, on the night he was betrayed and began his saving passion,[8] he instituted the sacrifice of the new covenant in his blood for the forgiveness of sins.[9] After his resurrection he sent the Holy Spirit upon the apostles, empowering them to forgive or retain sins[10] and sending

[1]See 2 Corinthians 5:18ff; Colossians 1:20.
[2]See John 8:34-36
[3]See 1 Peter 2:9.
[4]See Luke 15.
[5]Luke 5:20, 27-32; 7:48.
[6]See Matthew 9:2-8.
[7]See Romans 4:25.
[8]See Roman Missal, Eucharistic Prayer II.
[9]See Matthew 26:28.
[10]See John 20:19-23.

them forth to all peoples to preach repentance and the forgiveness of sins in his name.[11]

The Lord said to Peter, "I will give you the keys of the kingdom of heaven, and whatever you bind on earth will be bound in heaven, and whatever you loose on earth will be loosed also in heaven" (Matthew 16:19). In obedience to this command, on the day of Pentecost Peter preached the forgiveness of sins by baptism: "Repent and let every one of you be baptized in the name of Jesus Christ for the forgiveness of your sins" (Acts 2:38).[12] Since then the Church has never failed to call men from sin to conversion and by the celebration of penance to show the victory of Christ over sin.

2. This victory is first brought to light in baptism where our fallen nature is crucified with Christ so that the body of sin may be destroyed and we may no longer be slaves to sin, but rise with Christ and live for God.[13] For this reason the Church proclaims its faith in "the one baptism for the forgiveness of sins."

In the sacrifice of the Mass the passion of Christ is made present; his body given for us and his blood shed for the forgiveness of sins are offered to God again by the Church for the salvation of the world. In the eucharist Christ is present and is offered as "the sacrifice which has made our peace"[14] with God and in order that "we may be brought together in unity"[15] by his Holy Spirit.

Furthermore our Savior Jesus Christ, when he gave to his apostles and their successors power to forgive sins, instituted in his Church the sacrament of penance. Thus the faithful who fall into sin after baptism may be reconciled with God and renewed in grace.[16] The Church "possesses both water and tears: the water of baptism, the tears of penance."[17]

[11]See Luke 24:47
[12]See Acts 3:19, 26; 17:30.
[13]See Romans 6:4-10.
[14]Roman Missal, Eucharistic Prayer III.
[15]Roman Missal, Eucharistic Prayer II.
[16]See Council of Trent, Session XIV, De sacramento Paenitentiae, Chapter I: Denz.-Schön. 1668 and 1670; can. 1: Denz.-Schön. 1701.
[17]St. Ambrose, Letter 41:12: PL 16, 1116.

II

THE RECONCILIATION OF PENITENTS IN THE CHURCH'S LIFE

THE CHURCH IS HOLY BUT ALWAYS IN NEED OF PURIFICATION

3. Christ "loved the Church and gave himself up for her to make her holy" (Ephesians 5:25-26), and he united the Church to himself as his bride.[18] He filled her with his divine gifts,[19] because she is his body and fullness, and through her he spreads truth and grace to all.

The members of the Church, however, are exposed to temptation and unfortunately often fall into sin. As a result, "while Christ, 'holy, innocent, and unstained' (Hebrews 7:26), did not know sin (2 Corinthians 5:21) but came only to atone for the sins of the people (see Hebrews 2:17), the Church, which includes within itself sinners and is at the same time holy and always in need of purification, constantly pursues repentance and renewal."[20]

PENANCE IN THE CHURCH'S LIFE AND LITURGY

4. The people of God accomplishes and perfects this continual repentance in many different ways. It shares in the suffering of Christ[21] by enduring its own difficulties, carries out works of mercy and charity,[22] and adopts ever more fully the outlook of the Gospel message. Thus the people of God becomes in the world a sign of conversion to God. All this the Church expresses in its life and celebrates in the liturgy when the faithful confess that they are sinners and ask pardon of God and of their brothers and sisters. This happens in penitential services, in the proclamation of the word of God, in prayer, and in the penitential aspects of the eucharistic celebration.[23]

[18]See Revelation 19:7.
[19]See Ephesians 1:22-23; Second Vatican Council, constitution *Lumen gentium*, no. 7: *AAS* 57 (1965) 9-11.
[20]Second Vatican Council, constitution *Lumen gentium*, no. 8: *ibid.*, 12.
[21]See 1 Peter 4:13.
[22]See 1 Peter 4:8.
[23]See Council of Trent, Session XIV, De sacramento Paenitentiae: Denz.-Schön. 1638, 1740, 1743; Congregation of Rites, instruction *Eucharisticum mysterium*, May 25, 1967, no. 35: *AAS* 59 (1967) 560-561; Roman Missal, *General Instruction*, nos. 29, 30, 56 a. b. g.

In the sacrament of penance the faithful "obtain from the
mercy of God pardon for their sins against him; at the same
time they are reconciled with the Church which they
wounded by their sins and which works for their conversion
by charity, example, and prayer."[24]

RECONCILIATION WITH GOD AND WITH THE CHURCH

5. Since every sin is an offense against God which disrupts
our friendship with him, "the ultimate purpose of penance
is that we should love God deeply and commit ourselves
completely to him."[25] Therefore, the sinner who by the
grace of a merciful God embraces the way of penance comes
back to the Father who "first loved us" (1 John 4:19), to
Christ who gave himself up for us,[26] and to the Holy Spirit
who has been poured out on us abundantly.[27]

"By the hidden and loving mystery of God's design men are
joined together in the bonds of supernatural solidarity, so
much so that the sin of one harms the others just as the
holiness of one benefits the others."[28] Penance always en-
tails reconciliation with our brothers and sisters who are
always harmed by our sins.

In fact, men frequently join together to commit injustice. It
is thus only fitting that they should help each other in doing
penance so that they who are freed from sin by the grace of
Christ may work with all men of good will for justice and
peace in the world.

THE SACRAMENT OF PENANCE AND ITS PARTS

6. The follower of Christ who has sinned but who has been
moved by the Holy Spirit to come to the sacrament of
penance should above all be converted to God with his
whole heart. This inner conversion of heart embraces sorrow
for sin and the intent to lead a new life. It is expressed

[24]Second Vatican Council, constitution *Lumen gentium*, no. 11: *AAS* 57
(1965) 15-16.
[25]Paul VI, Apostolic Constitution *Paenitemini*, February 17, 1966: *AAS* 58
(1966) 179; See Second Vatican Council, constitution *Lumen gentium*, no.
11: AAS 57 (1965) 15-16.
[26]See Galatians 2:20; Ephesians 5:25.
[27]See Titus 3:6.
[28]Paul VI, Apostolic Constitution *Indulgentiarum doctrina*, January 1, 1967,
no. 4: *AAS* 59 (1967) 9; see Pius XII, encyclical *Mystici Corporis*, June 29,
1943: *AAS* 35 (1943) 213.

through confession made to the Church, due satisfaction, and amendment of life. God grants pardon for sin through the Church, which works by the ministry of priests.[29]

a) Contrition

The most important act of the penitent is contrition, which is "heartfelt sorrow and aversion for the sin committed along with the intention of sinning no more."[30] "We can only approach the Kingdom of Christ by *metanoia*. This is a profound change of the whole person by which one begins to consider, judge, and arrange his life according to the holiness and love of God, made manifest in his Son in the last days and given to us in abundance" (see Hebrews 1:2; Colossians 1:19 and *passim*).[31] The genuineness of penance depends on this heartfelt contrition. For conversion should affect a person from within so that it may progressively enlighten him and render him continually more like Christ.

b) Confession

The sacrament of penance includes the confession of sins, which comes from true knowledge of self before God and from contrition for those sins. However, this inner examination of heart and the exterior accusation should be made in the light of God's mercy. Confession requires in the penitent the will to open his heart to the minister of God, and in the minister a spiritual judgment by which, acting in the person of Christ, he pronounces his decision of forgiveness or retention of sins in accord with the power of the keys.[32]

c) Act of Penance (Satisfaction)

True conversion is completed by acts of penance or satisfaction for the sins committed, by amendment of conduct, and also by the reparation of injury.[33] The kind and extent of the

[29]See Council of Trent, Session XIV, De sacramento Paenitentiae, Chapter I: Denz.-Schön. 1673-1675.
[30]*Ibid.*, Chapter 4: Denz.-Schön. 1676.
[31]Paul VI, Apostolic Constitution *Paenitemini*, February 17, 1966: *AAS* 58 (1966) 179.
[32]See Council of Trent, Session XIV, De sacramento Paenitentiae, Chapter 5: Denz.-Schön. 1679.
[33]See Council of Trent, Session XIV, De sacramento Paenitentiae, Chapter 8: Denz.-Schön. 1690-1692; Paul VI, Apostolic Constitution *Indulgentiarum doctrina*, January 1, 1967, nos. 2-3: *AAS* 59 (1967) 6-8.

satisfaction should be suited to the personal condition of each penitent so that each one may restore the order which he disturbed and through the corresponding remedy be cured of the sickness from which he suffered. Therefore, it is necessary that the act of penance really be a remedy for sin and a help to renewal of life. Thus the penitent, "forgetting the things which are behind him" (Philippians 3:13), again becomes part of the mystery of salvation and turns himself toward the future.

d) Absolution

Through the sign of absolution God grants pardon to the sinner who in sacramental confession manifests his change of heart to the Church's minister, and thus the sacrament of penance is completed. In God's design the humanity and loving kindness of our Savior have visibly appeared to us,[34] and God uses visible signs to give salvation and to renew the broken covenant.

In the sacrament of penance the Father receives the repentant son who comes back to him, Christ places the lost sheep on his shoulders and brings it back to the sheepfold, and the Holy Spirit sanctifies this temple of God again or lives more fully within it. This is finally expressed in a renewed and more fervent sharing of the Lord's table, and there is great joy at the banquet of God's Church over the son who has returned from afar.[35]

THE NECESSITY AND BENEFIT OF THE SACRAMENT

7. Just as the wound of sin is varied and multiple in the life of individuals and of the community, so too the healing which penance provides is varied. Those who by grave sin have withdrawn from the communion of love with God are called back in the sacrament of penance to the life they have lost. And those who through daily weakness fall into venial sins draw strength from a repeated celebration of penance to gain the full freedom of the children of God.

a) To obtain the saving remedy of the sacrament of penance, according to the plan of our merciful God, the faithful

[34]See Titus 3:4-5.
[35]See Luke 15:7, 10, 32.

must confess to a priest each and every grave sin which they remember upon examination of their conscience.[36]

b) Moreover, frequent and careful celebration of this sacrament is also very useful as a remedy for venial sins. This is not a mere ritual repetition or psychological exercise, but a serious striving to perfect the grace of baptism so that, as we bear in our body the death of Jesus Christ, his life may be seen in us ever more clearly.[37] In confession of this kind, penitents who accuse themselves of venial faults should try to conform more closely to Christ and to follow the voice of the Spirit more attentively.

In order that this sacrament of healing may truly achieve its purpose among Christ's faithful, it must take root in their whole lives and move them to more fervent service of God and neighbor.

The celebration of this sacrament is thus always an act in which the Church proclaims its faith, gives thanks to God for the freedom with which Christ has made us free,[38] and offers its life as a spiritual sacrifice in praise of God's glory, as it hastens to meet the Lord Jesus.

III. OFFICES AND MINISTRIES IN THE RECONCILIATION OF PENITENTS

THE COMMUNITY IN THE CELEBRATION OF PENANCE

8. The whole Church, as a priestly people, acts in different ways in the work of reconciliation which has been entrusted to it by the Lord. Not only does the Church call sinners to repentance by preaching the word of God, but it also intercedes for them and helps penitents with maternal care and solicitude to acknowledge and admit their sins and so obtain the mercy of God who alone can forgive sins. Furthermore, the Church becomes the instrument of the conversion and absolution of the penitent through the ministry entrusted by Christ to the apostles and their successors.[39]

[36]See Council of Trent, Session XIV, De sacramento Paenitentiae, can. 7-8: Denz.-Schön. 1707-1708.
[37]See 2 Corinthians 4:10.
[38]See Galatians 4:31.
[39]See Matthew 18:18; John 20:23.

THE MINISTER OF THE SACRAMENT OF PENANCE

9. a) The Church exercises the ministry of the sacrament of penance through bishops and priests. By preaching God's word they call the faithful to conversion; in the name of Christ and by the power of the Holy Spirit they declare and grant the forgiveness of sins.

In the exercise of this ministry priests act in communion with the bishop and share in his power and office of regulating the penitential discipline.[40]

b) The competent minister of the sacrament of penance is a priest who has the faculty to absolve in accordance with canon law. All priests, however, even though not approved to hear confessions, absolve validly and licitly all penitents who are in danger of death.

THE PASTORAL EXERCISE OF THIS MINISTRY

10. a) In order to fulfill his ministry properly and faithfully the confessor should understand the disorders of souls and apply the appropriate remedies to them. He should fulfill his office of judge wisely and should acquire the knowledge and prudence necessary for this task by serious study, guided by the teaching authority of the Church and especially by fervent prayer to God. Discernment of spirits is a deep knowledge of God's action in the hearts of men; it is a gift of the Spirit as well as the fruit of charity.[41]

b) The confessor should always be ready and willing to hear the confessions of the faithful when they make a reasonable request of him.[42]

c) By receiving the repentant sinner and leading him to the light of the truth the confessor fulfills a paternal function: he reveals the heart of the Father and shows the image of Christ the Good Shepherd. He should keep in mind that he has been entrusted with the ministry of Christ, who mercifully accomplished the saving work of man's redemption and who is present by his power in the sacraments.[43]

[40]See Second Vatican Council, constitution *Lumen gentium*, no. 26: *AAS* 57 (1965) 31-32.
[41]See Philippians 1:9-10.
[42]See Congregation for the Doctrine of the Faith, *Normae pastorales circa absolutionem sacramentalem generali modo impertiendam*, June 16, 1972, No. XII: *AAS* 64 (1972) 514.
[43]See Second Vatican Council, constitution *Sacrosanctum Concilium*, no. 7: *AAS* 56 (1964) 100-101.

d) As the minister of God the confessor comes to know the secrets of another's conscience, and he is bound to keep the sacramental seal of confession absolutely inviolate.

THE PENITENT

11. The acts of the penitent in the celebration of the sacrament are of the greatest importance.

When with proper dispositions he approaches this saving remedy instituted by Christ and confesses his sins, he shares by his actions in the sacrament itself; the sacrament is completed when the words of absolution are spoken by the minister in the name of Christ.

Thus the faithful Christian, as he experiences and proclaims the mercy of God in his life, celebrates with the priest the liturgy by which the Church continually renews itself.

IV
THE CELEBRATION OF THE SACRAMENT OF PENANCE

THE PLACE OF CELEBRATION

12. The sacrament of penance is celebrated in the place and location prescribed by law.

THE TIME OF CELEBRATION

13. The reconciliation of penitents may be celebrated at any time on any day, but it is desirable that the faithful know the day and time at which the priest is available for this ministry. They should be encouraged to approach the sacrament of penance at times when Mass is not being celebrated and especially during the scheduled periods.[44]

The season of Lent is most appropriate for celebrating the sacrament of penance. Already on Ash Wednesday the people of God has heard the solemn invitation "Turn away from sin and believe the good news." It is therefore fitting to have several penitential celebrations during Lent, so that all the faithful may have an opportunity to be reconciled with

[44]See Congregation of Rites, instruction Eucharisticum mysterium, May 25, 1967, no. 35: AAS 59 (1967) 560-561.

God and their neighbor and so be able to celebrate the
paschal mystery in the Easter triduum with renewed hearts.

LITURGICAL VESTMENTS

14. The regulations laid down by the local Ordinaries for
the use of liturgical vestments in the celebration of penance
are to be observed.

A
RITE FOR THE RECONCILIATION OF
INDIVIDUAL PENITENTS

PREPARATION OF PRIEST AND PENITENT

15. Priest and penitent should first prepare themselves by
prayer to celebrate the sacrament. The priest should call
upon the Holy Spirit so that he may receive enlightenment
and charity. The penitent should compare his life with the
example and commandments of Christ and then pray to
God for the forgiveness of his sins.

WELCOMING THE PENITENT

16. The priest should welcome the penitent with fraternal
charity and, if the occasion permits, address him with
friendly words. The penitent then makes the sign of the
cross, saying: **In the name of the Father, and of the Son, and
of the Holy Spirit. Amen.** The priest may also make the sign
of the cross with the penitent. Next the priest briefly urges
the penitent to have confidence in God. If the penitent is
unknown to the priest, it is proper for him to indicate his
state in life, the time of his last confession, his difficulties in
leading the Christian life, and anything else which may help
the confessor in exercising his ministry.

READING THE WORD OF GOD

17. Then the priest, or the penitent himself, may read a text
of holy Scripture, or this may be done as part of the
preparation for the sacrament. Through the word of God the
Christian receives light to recognize his sins and is called to
conversion and to confidence in God's mercy.

CONFESSION OF SINS AND THE ACT OF PENANCE

18. The penitent then confesses his sins, beginning, where customary, with a form of general confession: **I confess to almighty God.** If necessary, the priest should help the penitent to make a complete confession; he should also encourage him to have sincere sorrow for his sins against God. Finally, the priest should offer suitable counsel to help the penitent begin a new life and, where necessary, instruct him in the duties of the Christian way of life.

If the penitent has been the cause of harm or scandal to others, the priest should lead him to resolve that he will make appropriate restitution.

Then the priest imposes an act of penance or satisfaction on the penitent; this should serve not only to make up for the past but also to help him to begin a new life and provide him with an antidote to weakness. As far as possible, the penance should correspond to the seriousness and nature of the sins. This act of penance may suitably take the form of prayer, self-denial, and especially service of one's neighbor and works of mercy. These will underline the fact that sin and its forgiveness have a social aspect.

THE PRAYER OF THE PENITENT AND THE ABSOLUTION BY THE PRIEST

19. After this the penitent manifests his contrition and resolution to begin a new life by means of a prayer for God's pardon. It is desirable that this prayer should be based on the words of Scripture.

Following this prayer, the priest extends his hands, or at least his right hand, over the head of the penitent and pronounces the formula of absolution, in which the essential words are: **I absolve you from your sins in the name of the Father, and of the Son, and of the Holy Spirit.** As he says the final words the priest makes the sign of the cross over the penitent. The form of absolution (see no. 46) indicates that the reconciliation of the penitent comes from the mercy of the Father; it shows the connection between the reconciliation of the sinner and the paschal mystery of Christ; it stresses the role of the Holy Spirit in the forgiveness of sins; finally, it underlines the ecclesial aspect of the sacrament because reconciliation with God is asked for and given through the ministry of the Church.

PROCLAMATION OF PRAISE AND DISMISSAL OF THE
PENITENT

20. After receiving pardon for his sins the penitent praises
the mercy of God and gives him thanks in a short invocation
taken from scripture. Then the priest tells him to go in
peace.

The penitent continues his conversion and expresses it by a
life renewed according to the Gospel and more and more
steeped in the love of God, for "love covers over a multitude
of sins" (1 Peter 4:8).

SHORT RITE

21. When pastoral need dictates it, the priest may omit or
shorten some parts of the rite but must always retain in their
entirety the confession of sins and the acceptance of the act
of penance, the invitation to contrition (no. 44), and the
form of absolution and the dismissal. In imminent danger of
death, it is sufficient for the priest to say the essential words
of the form of absolution, namely, **I absolve you from your
sins in the name of the Father, and of the Son, and of the
Holy Spirit.**

B
RITE FOR RECONCILIATION OF SEVERAL
PENITENTS WITH INDIVIDUAL
CONFESSION AND ABSOLUTION

22. When a number of penitents assemble at the same time
to receive sacramental reconciliation, it is fitting that they be
prepared for the sacrament by a celebration of the word of
God.

Those who will receive the sacrament at another time may
also take part in the service.

Communal celebration shows more clearly the ecclesial nature of penance. The faithful listen together to the word of
God, which proclaims his mercy and invites them to conversion; at the same time they examine the conformity of their
lives with that word of God and help each other through
common prayer. After each person has confessed his sins
and received absolution, all praise God together for his
wonderful deeds on behalf of the people he has gained for
himself through the blood of his Son.

If necessary, several priests should be available in suitable places to hear individual confessions and to reconcile the penitents.

INTRODUCTORY RITES

23. When the faithful are assembled, a suitable hymn may be sung. Then the priest greets them, and, if necessary, he or another minister gives a brief introduction to the celebration and explains the order of service. Next he invites all to pray and after a period of silence completes the (opening) prayer.

THE CELEBRATION OF THE WORD OF GOD

24. The sacrament of penance should begin with a hearing of God's word, because through his word God calls men to repentance and leads them to a true conversion of heart.

One or more readings may be chosen. If more than one are read, a psalm, another suitable song, or a period of silence should be inserted between them, so that the word of God may be more deeply understood and heartfelt assent may be given to it. If there is only one reading, it is preferable that it be from the gospel.

Readings should be chosen which illustrate the following:
   a) the voice of God calling men back to conversion and ever closer conformity with Christ;
   b) the mystery of our reconciliation through the death and resurrection of Christ and through the gift of the Holy Spirit;
   c) the judgment of God about good and evil in men's lives as a help in the examination of conscience.

25. The homily, taking its theme from the scriptural text, should lead the penitents to examine their consciences and to turn away from sin and toward God. It should remind the faithful that sin works against God, against the community and one's neighbors, and against the sinner himself. Therefore, it would be good to recall:
   a) the infinite mercy of God, greater than all our sins, by which again and again he calls us back to himself;
   b) the need for interior repentance, by which we are genuinely prepared to make reparation for sin;
   c) the social aspect of grace and sin, by which the actions of individuals in some degree affect the whole body of the Church;

d) the duty to make satisfaction for sin, which is effective because of Christ's work of reparation and requires especially, in addition to works of penance, the exercise of true charity toward God and neighbor.

26. After the homily a suitable period of silence should be allowed for examining one's conscience and awakening true contrition for sin. The priest or a deacon or other minister may help the faithful with brief considerations or a litany, adapted to their background, age, etc.

If it is judged suitable, this communal examination of conscience and awakening of contrition may take the place of the homily. But in this case it should be clearly based on the text of scripture that has just been read.

THE RITE OF RECONCILIATION

27. At the invitation of the deacon or other minister, all kneel or bow their heads and say a form of general confession (for example, **I confess to almighty God**). Then they stand and join in a litany or suitable song to express confession of sins, heartfelt contrition, prayer for forgiveness, and trust in God's mercy. Finally, they say the Lord's Prayer, which is never omitted.

28. After the Lord's Prayer the priests go to the places assigned for confession. The penitents who desire to confess their sins go to the priest of their choice. After receiving a suitable act of penance, they are absolved by him with the form for the reconciliation of an individual penitent.

29. When the confessions are over, the priests return to the sanctuary. The priest who presides invites all to make an act of thanksgiving and to praise God for his mercy. This may be done in a psalm or hymn or litany. Finally, the priest concludes the celebration with prayer, praising God for the great love he has shown us.

DISMISSAL OF THE PEOPLE

30. After the prayer of thanksgiving the priest blesses the faithful. Then the deacon or the priest himself dismisses the congregation.

C
RITE FOR RECONCILIATION OF PENITENTS WITH GENERAL CONFESSION AND ABSOLUTION

THE DISCIPLINE OF GENERAL ABSOLUTION

31. Individual, integral confession and absolution remain the only ordinary way for the faithful to reconcile themselves with God and the Church, unless physical or moral impossibility excuses from this kind of confession.

Particular, occasional circumstances may render it lawful and even necessary to give general absolution to a number of penitents without their previous individual confession.

In addition to cases involving danger of death, it is lawful to give sacramental absolution to several of the faithful at the same time, after they have made only a generic confession but have been suitably called to repentance, if there is grave need, namely when, in view of the number of penitents, sufficient confessors are not available to hear individual confessions properly within a suitable period of time, so that the penitents would, through no fault of their own, have to go without sacramental grace or holy communion for a long time. This may happen especially in mission territories but in other places as well and also in groups of persons when the need is established.

General absolution is not lawful, when confessors are available, for the sole reason of the large number of penitents, as may be on the occasion of some major feast or pilgrimage.[45]

32. The judgment about the presence of the above conditions and the decision concerning the lawfulness of giving general sacramental absolution are reserved to the bishop of the diocese, who is to consult with the other members of the episcopal conference.

Over and above the cases determined by the dioscesan bishop, if any other serious need arises for giving sacramental absolution to several persons together, the priest must have recourse to the local Ordinary beforehand, when this is

[45]Congregation for the Doctrine of the Faith, *Normae pastorales circa absolutionem sacramentalem generali modo impertiendam*, June 16, 1972, no. III: *AAS* 64 (1972) 511.

possible, if he is to give absolution lawfully. Otherwise, he should inform the Ordinary as soon as possible of the need and of the absolution which he gave.[46]

33. In order that the faithful may profit from sacramental absolution given to several persons at the same time, it is absolutely necessary that they be properly disposed. Each one should be sorry for his sins and resolve to avoid committing them again. He should intend to repair any scandal and harm he may have caused and likewise resolve to confess in due time each one of the grave sins which he cannot confess at present. These dispositions and conditions, which are required for the validity of the sacrament, should be carefully recalled to the faithful by priests.[47]

34. Those who receive pardon for grave sins by a common absolution should go to individual confession before they receive this kind of absolution again, unless they are impeded by a just reason. They are strictly bound, unless this is morally impossible, to go to confession within a year. The precept which obliges each of the faithful to confess at least once a year to a priest all the grave sins which he has not individually confessed before also remains in force in this case too.[48]

THE RITE OF GENERAL ABSOLUTION

35. For the reconciliation of penitents by general confession and absolution in the cases provided by law, everything takes place as described above for the reconciliation of several penitents with individual confession and absolution, with the following exceptions:

a) After the homily or during it, the faithful who seek general absolution should be instructed to dispose themselves properly, that is, each one should be sorry for his sins and resolve to avoid committing them again. He should intend to repair any scandal and harm he may have caused and likewise resolve to confess in due time each one of the grave sins which cannot be confessed at present.[49] Some act of penance should be proposed for all; individuals may add to this penance if they wish.

[46]Ibid., no. V: loc. cit., 512.
[47]Ibid., nos. VI and XI: loc. cit., 512, 514.
[48]Ibid., nos. VII and VIII: loc. cit, 512-513.
[49]See Ibid., no. VI: loc. cit., 512.

b) The deacon, another minister, or the priest then calls upon the penitents who wish to receive absolution to show their intention by some sign (for example, by bowing their heads, kneeling, or giving some other sign determined by the episcopal conferences). They should also say together a form of general confession (for example, **I confess to almighty God**), which may be followed by a litany or a penitential song. Then the Lord's Prayer is sung or said by all, as indicated in no. 27, above.

c) Then the priest calls upon the grace of the Holy Spirit for the forgiveness of sins, proclaims the victory over sin of Christ's death and resurrection, and gives sacramental absolution to the penitents.

d) Finally, the priest invites the people to give thanks, as described in no. 29, above, and, omitting the concluding prayer, he immediately blesses and dismisses them.

V
PENITENTIAL CELEBRATIONS

NATURE AND STRUCTURE

36. Penitential celebrations are gatherings of the people of God to hear the proclamation of God's word. This invites them to conversion and renewal of life and announces our freedom from sin through the death and resurrection of Christ. The structure of these services is the same as that usually followed in celebrations of the word of God[50] and given in *Rite for Reconciliation of Several Penitents*.

It is appropriate, therefore, that after the introductory rites (song, greeting, and prayer) one or more biblical readings be chosen with songs, psalms, or periods of silence inserted between them. In the homily these readings should be explained and applied to the congregation. Before or after the readings from scripture, readings from the Fathers or other writers may be selected which will help the community and each person to a true awareness of sin and heartfelt sorrow, in other words. to bring about conversion of life.

After the homily and reflection on God's word, it is desirable that the congregation, united in voice and spirit, pray

---

[50]See Congregation of Rites, instruction *Inter Oecumenici*, September 26, 1964, nos. 37-39: *AAS* 56 (1964) 110-111.

together in a litany or in some other way suited to general participation. At the end the Lord's Prayer is said, asking God our Father **to forgive us our sins as we forgive those who sin against us . . . and deliver us from evil.** The priest or the minister who presides concludes with a prayer and the dismissal of the people.

BENEFIT AND IMPORTANCE

37. Care should be taken that the faithful do not confuse these celebrations with the celebration of the sacrament of penance.[51] Penitential celebrations are very helpful in promoting conversion of life and purification of heart.[52]

It is desirable to arrange such services especially for these purposes:
—to foster the spirit of penance within the Christian community;
—to help the faithful to prepare for confession which can be made individually later at a convenient time;
—to help children gradually to form their conscience about sin in human life and about freedom from sin through Christ;
—to help catechumens during their conversion.

Penitential celebrations, moreover, are very useful in places where no priest is available to give sacramental absolution. They offer help in reaching that perfect contrition which comes from charity and enables the faithful to attain to God's grace through a desire for the sacrament of penance.[53]

VI
ADAPTATIONS OF THE RITE
TO VARIOUS REGIONS AND CIRCUMSTANCES

ADAPTATIONS BY THE EPISCOPAL CONFERENCES

38. In preparing particular rituals episcopal conferences may adapt the rite of penance to the needs of individual regions

[51]See Congregation for the Doctrine of the Faith, *Normae pastorales circa absolutionem sacramentalem generali modo impertiendam*, June 16, 1972, no. X: *AAS* 64 (1972) 513-514.
[52]*Ibid.*
[53]See Council of Trent, Session XIV, De sacramento Paenitentiae, chapter 5: Denz.-Schön. 1677.

so that after confirmation by the Apostolic See the rituals may be used in the respective regions. It is the responsibility of episcopal conferences in this matter:

a) to establish regulations for the discipline of the sacrament of penance, particularly those affecting the ministry of priests and the reservation of sins;

b) to determine more precise regulations about the place proper for the ordinary celebration of the sacrament of penance and about the signs of penance to be shown by the faithful before general absolution (see no. 23, above);

c) to prepare translations of texts adapted to the character and language of each people and also to compose new texts for the prayers of the faithful and the minister, keeping intact the sacramental form.

THE COMPETENCE OF THE BISHOP

39. It is for the diocesan bishop:

a) to regulate the discipline of penance in his diocese,[54] including adaptations of the rite according to the rules proposed by the episcopal conference;

b) to determine, after consultation with the other members of the episcopal conference, when general sacramental absolution may be permitted under the conditions laid down by the Holy See.[55]

ADAPTATIONS BY THE MINISTER

40. It is for priests, and especially parish priests:

a) in reconciling individuals or the community, to adapt the rite to the concrete circumstances of the penitents. The essential structure and the entire form of absolution must be kept, but if necessary they may omit some parts for pastoral reasons or enlarge upon them, may select the texts of readings or prayers, and may choose a place more suitable for the celebration according to the regulations of the episcopal conference, so that the entire celebration may be rich and fruitful;

b) to propose and prepare occasional penitential celebrations during the year, especially in Lent. In order that the

[54]See Second Vatican Council, constitution *Lumen gentium*, no. 26: *AAS* 57 (1965) 31-32.
[55]See Congregation for the Doctrine of the Faith, *Normae pastorales circa absolutionem sacramentalem generali modo impertiendam*, no. V: *AAS* 64 (1972), 512.

texts chosen and the order of the celebration may be adapted to the conditions and circumstances of the community or group (for example, children, sick persons, etc.), they may be assisted by others, including the laity;

c) to decide to give general sacramental absolution preceded by only a generic confession, when a grave necessity not foreseen by the diocesan bishop arises and when recourse to him is not possible. They are obliged to notify the Ordinary as soon as possible of the need and of the fact that absolution was given.

CHAPTER I

RITE FOR RECONCILIATION
OF
INDIVIDUAL PENITENTS

RECEPTION OF THE PENITENT

41. When the penitent comes to confess his sins, the priest welcomes him warmly and greets him with kindness.

42. Then the penitent makes the sign of the cross which the priest may make also.

In the name of the Father, and of the Son, and of the Holy Spirit. Amen.

The priest invites the penitent to have trust in God, in these or similar words:

**May God, who has enlightened every heart,
help you to know your sins
and trust in his mercy.**
The penitent answers: **Amen.**

Or Ezekiel 33:11 [67]:
**The Lord does not wish the sinner to die
but to turn back to him and live.
Come before him with trust in his mercy.**

Or Luke 5:32 [68]:
**May the Lord Jesus welcome you.
He came to call sinners, not the just.
Have confidence in him.**

Or [69]:
**May the grace of the Holy Spirit
fill your heart with light,
that you may confess your sins with loving trust
and come to know that God is merciful.**

Or [70]:
**May the Lord be in your heart
and help you to confess your sins with true sorrow.**

Or 1 John 2:1-2 [71]:
**If you have sinned, do not lose heart.
We have Jesus Christ to plead for us with the Father:
he is the holy One,
the atonement for our sins
and for the sins of the whole world.**

READING OF THE WORD OF GOD (OPTIONAL)

43. Then the priest may read or say from memory a text of Scripture which proclaims God's mercy and calls man to conversion.

Ezekiel 11:19-20 [73]

Let us listen to the Lord as he speaks to us:

I will give them a single heart
  and I will put a new spirit in them;
I will remove the heart of stone from their bodies
  and give them a heart of flesh instead,
    so that they will keep my laws and respect my observances
    and put them into practice.
Then they shall be my people and I will be their God.

Matthew 6:14-15 [74]

Let us listen to the Lord as he speaks to us:

Yes, if you forgive others their failings,
your heavenly Father will forgive you yours;
but if you do not forgive others,
your Father will not forgive your failings either.

Mark 1:14-15 [75]

After John had been arrested, Jesus went into Galilee.
There he proclaimed the Good News from God.
"The time has come," he said,
  "and the kingdom of God is close at hand.
Repent, and believe the Good News."

Romans 5:8-9 [79]

What proves that God loves us is
  that Christ died for us while we were still sinners.
Having died to make us righteous, is it likely
  that he would now fail to save us from God's anger?

Ephesians 5:1-2 [80]

**Try to imitate God, as children of his that he loves,
and follow Christ by loving as he loved you,
giving himself up in our place
as a fragrant offering and a sacrifice to God.**

1 John 1:6-7, 9 [83]

**If we say that we are in union with God
while we are living in darkness,
we are lying because we are not living the truth.
But if we live our lives in the light,
as he is in the light,
we are in union with one another,
and the blood of Jesus, his Son,
purifies us from all sin.
But if we acknowledge our sins,
then God who is faithful and just
will forgive our sins and purify us
from everything that is wrong.**

A reading may also be chosen from those given in nos. 72-83 and 101-201 for the reconciliation of several penitents. The priest and penitent may choose other readings from scripture. [84]

CONFESSION OF SINS AND ACCEPTANCE OF SATISFACTION

44. Where it is the custom, the penitent says a general formula for confession (for example, **I confess to almighty God**) before he confesses his sins.

If necessary, the priest helps the penitent to make an integral confession and gives him suitable counsel. He urges him to be sorry for his faults, reminding him that through the sacrament of penance the Christian dies and rises with Christ and is thus renewed in the paschal mystery. The priest proposes an act of penance which the penitent accepts to make satisfaction for sin and to amend his life.

The priest should make sure that he adapts his counsel to the penitent's circumstances.

PRAYER OF THE PENITENT AND ABSOLUTION

45. The priest then asks the penitent to express his sorrow, which the penitent may do in these or similar words:

**My God,
I am sorry for my sins with all my heart.
In choosing to do wrong
and failing to do good,
I have sinned against you
whom I should love above all things.
I firmly intend, with your help,
to do penance,
to sin no more,
and to avoid whatever leads me to sin.
Our Savior Jesus Christ
suffered and died for us.
In his name, my God, have mercy.**

Or Psalm 24:6-7 [85]:
**Remember, Lord, your compassion and mercy which
you showed long ago.
Do not recall the sins and failings of my youth.
In your mercy remember me, Lord, because of your
goodness.**

Or Psalm 50:4-5 [86]:
**Wash me from my guilt
and cleanse me of my sin.
I acknowledge my offense;
my sin is before me always.**

Or Luke 15:18; 18:13 [87]:
**Father, I have sinned against you
and am not worthy to be called your son.
Be merciful to me, a sinner.**

Or [88]:
**Father of mercy,
like the prodigal son
I return to you and say:**

"I have sinned against you
and am no longer worthy to be called your son."
Christ Jesus, Savior of the world,
I pray with the repentant thief
to whom you promised Paradise:
"Lord, remember me in your kingdom."
Holy Spirit, fountain of love,
I call on you with trust:
"Purify my heart,
and help me to walk as a child of light."

Or [89]:
Lord Jesus,
you opened the eyes of the blind,
healed the sick,
forgave the sinful woman,
and after Peter's denial confirmed him in your love.
Listen to my prayer:
forgive all my sins,
renew your love in my heart,
help me to live in perfect unity with my fellow
    Christians
that I may proclaim your saving power to all the
    world.

Or [90]:
Lord Jesus,
you chose to be called the friend of sinners.
By your saving death and resurrection
free me from my sins.
May your peace take root in my heart
and bring forth a harvest
of love, holiness, and truth.

Or [91]:
Lord Jesus Christ,
you are the Lamb of God;
you take away the sins of the world.
Through the grace of the Holy Spirit
restore me to friendship with your Father,

cleanse me from every stain of sin
in the blood you shed for me,
and raise me to new life
for the glory of your name.

Or [92]:
Lord God,
in your goodness have mercy on me:
do not look on my sins,
but take away all my guilt.
Create in me a clean heart
and renew within me an upright spirit.

Or:
Lord Jesus, Son of God
have mercy on me, a sinner.

46. Then the priest extends his hands over the penitent's head (or at least extends his right hand) and says:

God, the Father of mercies,
through the death and resurrection of his Son
has reconciled the world to himself
and sent the Holy Spirit among us
for the forgiveness of sins;
through the ministry of the Church
may God give you pardon and peace,

and I absolve you from your sins
in the name of the Father, and of the Son, ✠
and of the Holy Spirit.
The penitent answers: Amen.

PROCLAMATION OF PRAISE OF GOD AND DISMISSAL

47. After the absolution, the priest continues:

Give thanks to the Lord, for he is good.
The penitent concludes: His mercy endures for ever.

Then the priest dismisses the penitent who has been
reconciled, saying:

The Lord has freed you from your sins. Go in peace.

Or [93]:
**May the Passion of our Lord Jesus Christ,
the intercession of the Blessed Virgin Mary,
    and of all the saints,
whatever good you do and suffering you endure,
heal your sins,
help you to grow in holiness,
and reward you with eternal life.
Go in peace.**

Or:
**The Lord has freed you from sin.
May he bring you safely to his kingdom in heaven.
Glory to him for ever.
R̹. Amen.**

Or:
**Blessed are those
whose sins have been forgiven,
whose evil deeds have been forgotten.
Rejoice in the Lord,
and go in peace.**

Or:
**Go in peace,
and proclaim to the world
the wonderful works of God
who has brought you salvation.**

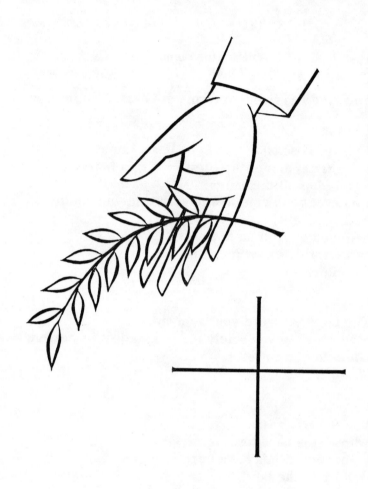

CHAPTER II

RITE FOR RECONCILIATION OF SEVERAL PENITENTS WITH INDIVIDUAL CONFESSION AND ABSOLUTION

INTRODUCTORY RITES

SONG

48. When the faithful have assembled, they may sing a psalm, antiphon, or other appropriate song while the priest is entering the church, for example:

Hear us, Lord,
for you are merciful and kind.
In your great compassion,
look on us with love.

Or:

Let us come with confidence before the throne of
grace
to receive God's mercy,
and we shall find pardon and strength
in our time of need.

GREETING

49. After the song the priest greets the congregation:
Grace, mercy, and peace be with you
from God the Father
and Christ Jesus our Savior.
R̲/. **And also with you.**

Or:

Grace and peace be with you
from God the Father
and from Jesus Christ
who loved us
and washed away our sins in his blood.
R̲/. **Glory to him for ever. Amen.**

Or [94]:
Grace, mercy, and peace
from God the Father and Jesus Christ his Son
be with you in truth and love.
R̲/. **Amen.**

Or [95]:
**May God open your hearts to his law
and give you peace;
may he answer your prayers
and restore you to friendship.
R̷. Amen.**

Or [96]:
**Grace and peace be with you
from God our Father
and from the Lord Jesus Christ
who laid down his life for our sins.
R̷. Glory to him for ever. Amen.**

Then the priest or another minister speaks briefly about the importance and purpose of the celebration and the order of the service.

OPENING PRAYER

50. The priest invites all to pray, using these or similar words:

Brothers and sisters, God calls us to conversion; let us therefore ask him for the grace of sincere repentance.

All pray in silence for a brief period. Then the priest sings or says the prayer:

**Lord,
hear the prayers of those who call on you,
forgive the sins of those who confess to you,
and in your merciful love
give us your pardon and your peace.
We ask this through Christ our Lord.
R̷. Amen.**

Or:
**Lord,
send your Spirit among us
to cleanse us in the waters of repentance.
May he make of us a living sacrifice
so that in every place,
by his life-giving power,**

we may praise your glory
and proclaim your loving compassion.
We ask this through Christ our Lord.
R̷. Amen.

Or [97]:
Lord,
turn to us in mercy
and forgive us all our sins
that we may serve you in true freedom.
We ask this through Christ our Lord.
R̷. Amen.

Or [98]:
Lord our God,
you are patient with sinners
and accept our desire to make amends.
We acknowledge our sins
and are resolved to change our lives.
Help us to celebrate this sacrament of your mercy
so that we may reform our lives
and receive from you the gift of everlasting joy.
We ask this through Christ our Lord.
R̷. Amen.

Or [99]:
Almighty and merciful God,
you have brought us together in the name of your Son
to receive your mercy and grace in our time of need.
Open our eyes to see the evil we have done.
Touch our hearts and convert us to yourself.
Where sin has divided and scattered,
may your love make one again;
where sin has brought weakness,
may your power heal and strengthen;
where sin has brought death,
may your Spirit raise to new life.

Give us a new heart to love you,
so that our lives may reflect the image of your Son.

May the world see the glory of Christ
revealed in your Church,
and come to know
that he is the one whom you have sent,
Jesus Christ, your Son, our Lord.
R̷. Amen.

Or [100]:
Father of mercies
and God of all consolation,
you do not wish the sinner to die
but to be converted and live.
Come to the aid of your people,
that they may turn from their sins
and live for you alone.
May we be attentive to your word,
confess our sins, receive your forgiveness,
and be always grateful for your loving kindness.
Help us to live the truth in love
and grow into the fullness of Christ, your Son,
who lives and reigns for ever and ever.
R̷. Amen.

CELEBRATION OF THE WORD OF GOD

51. The celebration of the word follows. If there are several
readings a psalm or other appropriate song or even a period
of silence should intervene between them, so that everyone
may understand the word of God more deeply and give it
his heartfelt assent. If there is only one reading, it is
preferable that it be from the gospel.

FIRST EXAMPLE

Love is the fullness of the law

FIRST READING:

Deuteronomy 5:1-3, 6-7, 11-12, 16-21a; 6:4-6   Love the Lord
your God with all your heart.

A reading from the book of Deuteronomy
Listen, Israel,

to the laws and customs that I proclaim in your hearing today.

Learn them and take care to observe them.

The Lord our God made a covenant with us at Horeb.
It was not with our fathers that the Lord made this covenant,
  but with us who are here, all living today.
He said:
"I am the Lord your God
  who brought you out of the land of Egypt,
  out of the house of slavery.
"You shall have no gods except me.
"You shall not utter the name of the Lord your God to misuse it,
  for the Lord will not leave unpunished
  the man who utters his name to misuse it.
"Observe the sabbath day and keep it holy,
  as the Lord your God has commanded you.
"Honor your father and your mother,
  as the Lord your God has commanded you,
  so that you may have long life and may prosper
  in the land that the Lord your God gives to you.
"You shall not kill.
"You shall not commit adultery.
"You shall not steal.
"You shall not bear false witness against your neighbor.
"You shall not covet your neighbor's wife."
Listen, Israel: the Lord our God is the one Lord.
You shall love the Lord your God with all your heart,
  with all your soul, with all your strength.
Let these words I urge on you today
  be written on your heart.
  This is the Word of the Lord.

RESPONSORIAL PSALM:

Baruch 1:15-22   Listen and have pity, Lord, because you are
merciful.

R̷. Listen and have pity, Lord, because you are merciful.

Integrity belongs to the Lord our God;
  to us the look of shame we wear today,
  because we have sinned in the sight of the Lord.   R̷.

We have disobeyed him.
We have not listened to the voice
   of the Lord our God telling us to follow the commandments
   which the Lord had ordained for us.
R̂. Listen and have pity, Lord, because you are merciful.

From the day when the Lord brought our ancestors
   out of the land of Egypt until today
   we have been disobedient to the Lord our God,
   we have been disloyal, refusing to listen to his voice.   R̂.

And so the disasters, and the curse
   which the Lord pronounced through his servant Moses
   the day he brought our fathers out of Egypt
   to give us a land where milk and honey flow,
   have seized on us, disasters we experience today.   R̂.

Despite all the words of those prophets whom he sent us,
   we have not listened to the voice of the Lord our God,
   but, each following the dictates of his evil heart,
   we have taken to serving alien gods,
   and doing what is displeasing to the Lord our God.   R̂.

SECOND READING:

Ephesians 5:1-14   Walk in love, as Christ loved us.

A reading from the letter of Paul to the Ephesians
Try to imitate God, as children of his that he loves,
   and follow Christ by loving as he loved you,
   giving himself up in our place
   as a fragrant offering and a sacrifice to God.
Among you there must be not even a mention
   of fornication or impurity in any of its forms,
   or promiscuity: this would hardly become the saints!
There must be no coarseness, or salacious talk and jokes—
   all this is wrong for you;
   raise your voices in thanksgiving instead.
For you can be quite certain that nobody who actually indulges
   in fornication or impurity or promiscuity—
   which is worshiping a false god—
   can inherit anything of the kingdom of God.
Do not let anyone deceive you with empty arguments:
   it is for this loose living that God's anger comes down
   on those who rebel against him.
Make sure that you are not included with them.

You were darkness once, but now you are light in the Lord;
   be like children of light, for the effects of the light
   are seen in complete goodness and right living and truth.
Try to discover what the Lord wants of you,
   having nothing to do with the futile works of darkness
   but exposing them by contrast.
The things which are done in secret
   are things that people are ashamed even to speak of;
   but anything exposed by the light will be illuminated
   and anything illuminated turns into light.
That is why it is said:
   Wake up from your sleep,
   rise from the dead,
   and Christ will shine on you.
   This is the Word of the Lord.

GOSPEL ACCLAMATION:

John 8:12

I am the light of the world.
The man who follows me will have the light of life.

GOSPEL:

Matthew 22:34-40   On these two commandments the whole
law and the prophets depend.

✝ A reading from the holy gospel according to Matthew

When the Pharisees heard that he had silenced
   the Sadducees they got together and, to disconcert him,
   one of them put a question,
   "Master, which is the greatest commandment of the Law?"
Jesus said,
   "You must love the Lord your God with all your heart,
   with all your soul, and with all your mind.
This is the greatest and the first commandment.
The second resembles it:
   You must love your neighbor as yourself.
On these two commandments hang the whole Law,
   and the Prophets also."
   This is the gospel of the Lord.

or: John 13:34-35; 15:10-13   I give you a new commandment:
love one another.

✢ A reading from the holy gospel according to John

Jesus said:
I give you a new commandment:
love one another;
just as I have loved you,
you also must love one another.
By this love you have for one another,
everyone will know that you are my disciples.

If you keep my commandments
you will remain in my love,
just as I have kept my Father's commandments
and remain in his love.
I have told you this
so that my own joy may be in you
and your joy be complete.
This is my commandment:
love one another,
as I have loved you.
A man can have no greater love
than to lay down his life for his friends.
This is the gospel of the Lord.

SECOND EXAMPLE

Your mind must be renewed

FIRST READING:

Isaiah 1:10-18   Stop doing what is wrong, and learn to do good.

A reading from the book of the prophet Isaiah

Hear the word of the Lord,
you rulers of Sodom;
listen to the command of our God,
you people of Gomorrah.

"What are your endless sacrifices to me?
says the Lord.
I am sick of holocausts of rams
and the fat of calves.
The blood of bulls and of goats revolts me.

When you come to present yourselves before me,
who asked you to trample over my courts?
Bring me your worthless offerings no more,
the smoke of them fills me with disgust.
New Moons, sabbaths, assemblies—
I cannot endure festival and solemnity.
Your New Moons and your pilgrimages
I hate with all my soul.
They lie heavy on me,
I am tired of bearing them.

When you stretch out your hands
I turn my eyes away.
You may multiply your prayers,
I shall not listen.
Your hands are covered with blood,
wash, make yourselves clean.

"Take your wrong-doing out of my sight.
Cease to do evil.
Learn to do good,
search for justice,
help the oppressed,
be just to the orphan,
plead for the widow."

"Come now, let us talk this over,
says the Lord.
Though your sins are like scarlet,
they shall be as white as snow;
though they are red as crimson,
they shall be like wool."
This is the Word of the Lord.

RESPONSORIAL PSALM:

Psalm 51:1-4, 8-17

℟. (19a) **A humbled heart is pleasing to God.**

**Have mercy on me, God, in your kindness.
In your compassion blot out my offence.
O wash me more and more from my guilt
and cleanse me from my sin.** ℟.

My offences truly I know them;
my sin is always before me.
Against you, you alone, have I sinned;
what is evil in your sight I have done.
℞. (19a) A humbled heart is pleasing to God.

Make me hear rejoicing and gladness,
that the bones you have crushed may revive.
From my sins turn away your face
and blot out all my guilt. ℞.

A pure heart create for me, O God,
put a steadfast spirit within me.
Do not cast me away from your presence,
nor deprive me of your holy spirit. ℞.

Give me again the joy of your help;
with a spirit of fervor sustain me,
that I may teach transgressors your ways
and sinners may return to you. ℞.

O rescue me, God my helper,
and my tongue shall ring out your goodness.
O Lord, open my lips
and my mouth shall declare your praise. ℞.

For in sacrifice you take no delight,
burnt offering from me you would refuse,
my sacrifice, a contrite spirit.
A humbled, contrite heart you will not spurn. ℞.

SECOND READING:

Ephesians 4:23-32 Your mind must be renewed by a spiritual revolution.

A reading from the letter of Paul to the Ephesians

Your mind must be renewed by a spiritual revolution
  so that you can put on the new self
  that has been created in God's way,
  in the goodness and holiness of the truth.

So from now on, there must be no more lies:
  You must speak the truth to one another,

since we are all parts of one another.
Even if you are angry, you must not sin:
  never let the sun set on your anger
  or else you will give the devil a foothold.
Anyone who was a thief must stop stealing:
  he should try to find some useful manual work instead,
  and be able to do some good by helping others that are in need.
Guard against foul talk;
  let your words be for the improvement of others,
  as occasion offers, and do good to your listeners,
  otherwise you will only be grieving the Holy Spirit of God
  who has marked you with his seal
  for you to be set free when the day comes.
Never have grudges against others, or lose your temper,
  or raise your voice to anybody, or call each other names,
  or allow any sort of spitefulness.
Be friends with one another, and kind,
  forgiving each other as readily as God forgave you in Christ.
  This is the Word of the Lord.

GOSPEL ACCLAMATION:

Matthew 11:28

Come to me, all you that labor and are burdened,
and I will give you rest.

GOSPEL:

Matthew 5:1-12   Happy the poor in spirit.

✛ A reading from the holy gospel according to Matthew

Seeing the crowds, [Jesus] went up the hill.
There he sat down and was joined by his disciples.
Then he began to speak. This is what he taught them:

  "How happy are the poor in spirit;
  theirs is the kingdom of heaven.
  Happy the gentle:
  they shall have the earth for their heritage.
  Happy those who mourn:
  they shall be comforted.
  Happy those who hunger and thirst for what is right:
  they shall be satisfied.

Happy the merciful:
they shall have mercy shown them.
Happy the pure in heart:
they shall see God.
Happy the peacemakers:
they shall be called sons of God.
Happy those who are persecuted in the cause of right:
theirs is the kingdom of heaven.

"Happy are you when people abuse you and persecute you
and speak all kinds of calumny against you on my account.
Rejoice and be glad, for your reward will be great in heaven;
this is how they persecuted the prophets before you."
This is the gospel of the Lord.

Other optional texts are given in nos. 101-201.

HOMILY

52. The homily which follows is based on the texts of the
readings and should lead the penitents to examine their
consciences and renew their lives.

EXAMINATION OF CONSCIENCE

53. A period of time may be spent in making an
examination of conscience and in arousing true sorrow for
sins. The priest, deacon, or another minister may help the
faithful by brief statements or a kind of litany, taking into
consideration their circumstances, age, etc.

RITE OF RECONCILIATION

GENERAL CONFESSION OF SINS

54. The deacon or another minister invites all to kneel or
bow, and to join in saying a general formula for confession
(for example, **I confess to almighty God**). Then they stand
and say a litany or sing an appropriate song. The Lord's
Prayer is always added at the end.

FIRST EXAMPLE

Deacon or Minister:
**My brothers and sisters, confess your sins and pray
for each other, that you may be healed.**

All say:

**I confess to almighty God,
and to you, my brothers and sisters,
that I have sinned through my own fault**

They strike their breast:

**in my thoughts and in my words,
in what I have done,
and in what I have failed to do;
and I ask blessed Mary, ever virgin,
all the angels and saints,
and you, my brothers and sisters,
to pray for me to the Lord our God.**

Deacon or minister:

**The Lord is merciful. He makes us clean of heart and
leads us out into his freedom when we acknowledge
our guilt. Let us ask him to forgive us and bind up the
wounds inflicted by our sins.**

Give us the grace of true repentance.
R̥. **We pray you, hear us.**

**Pardon your servants and release them from the debt
of sin.**
R̥. **We pray you, hear us.**

**Forgive your children who confess their sins, and
restore them to full communion with your Church.**
R̥. **We pray you, hear us.**

**Renew the glory of baptism in those who have lost it
by sin.**
R̥. **We pray you, hear us.**

**Welcome them to your altar, and renew their spirit
with the hope of eternal glory.**
R̥. **We pray you, hear us.**

**Keep them faithful to your sacraments and loyal in
your service.**
R̥. **We pray you, hear us.**

Renew your love in their hearts, and make them bear

witness to it in their daily lives.
R̂. **We pray you, hear us.**

**Keep them always obedient to your commandments
and protect within them your gift of eternal life.**
R̂. **We pray you, hear us.**

Deacon or minister:
**Let us now pray to God our Father in the words Christ
gave us, and ask him for his forgiveness and
protection from all evil.**

All say together:
Our Father . . .

The priest concludes:
**Lord,
draw near to your servants
who in the presence of your Church
confess that they are sinners.
Through the ministry of the Church
free them from all sin
so that renewed in spirit
they may give you thankful praise.
We ask this through Christ our Lord.**
R̂. **Amen.**

SECOND EXAMPLE

Deacon or minister:
**Brothers and sisters, let us call to mind the goodness
of God our Father, and acknowledge our sins, so that
we may receive his merciful forgiveness.**

All say:
**I confess to almighty God,
and to you, my brothers and sisters,
that I have sinned through my own fault**

They strike their breast:
**in my thoughts and in my words,
in what I have done,**

and in what I have failed to do;
and I ask blessed Mary, ever virgin,
all the angels and saints,
and you, my brothers and sisters,
to pray for me to the Lord our God.

Deacon or minister:
Christ our Savior is our advocate with the Father:
with humble hearts let us ask him to forgive us our
    sins
and cleanse us from every stain.

You were sent with good news for the poor and
    healing for the contrite.
R̰. Lord, be merciful to me, a sinner. Or: Lord, have mercy.

You came to call sinners, not the just.
R̰. Lord, be merciful to me, a sinner. Or: Lord, have mercy.

You forgave the many sins of the woman who showed
you great love.
R̰. Lord, be merciful to me, a sinner. Or: Lord, have mercy.

You did not shun the company of outcasts and sinners.
R̰. Lord, be merciful to me, a sinner. Or: Lord, have mercy.

You carried back to the fold the sheep that had
strayed.
R̰. Lord, be merciful to me, a sinner. Or: Lord, have mercy.

You did not condemn the woman taken in adultery,
but sent her away in peace.
R̰. Lord, be merciful to me, a sinner. Or: Lord, have mercy.

You called Zacchaeus to repentance and a new life.
R̰. Lord, be merciful to me, a sinner. Or: Lord, have mercy.

You promised Paradise to the repentant thief.

℟. **Lord, be merciful to me, a sinner.** Or: **Lord, have mercy.**

You are always interceding for us at the right hand of the Father.
℟. **Lord, be merciful to me, a sinner.** Or: **Lord, have mercy.**

Deacon or minister:
Now, in obedience to Christ himself, let us join in prayer to the Father, asking him to forgive us as we forgive others.

All say together:
Our Father . . .

The priest concludes:
**Father, our source of life,
you know our weakness.
May we reach out with joy to grasp your hand
and walk more readily in your ways.
We ask this through Christ our Lord.**
℟. **Amen.**

For other texts see numbers 202-205, pages 140-148.

INDIVIDUAL CONFESSION AND ABSOLUTION

55. Then the penitents go to the priests designated for individual confession, and confess their sins. Each one receives and accepts a fitting act of satisfaction and is absolved. After hearing the confession and offering suitable counsel, the priest extends his hands over the penitent's head (or at least extends his right hand) and gives him absolution. Everything else which is customary in individual confession is omitted.

**God, the Father of mercies,
through the death and resurrection of his Son
has reconciled the world to himself
and sent the Holy Spirit among us
for the forgiveness of sins;
through the ministry of the Church
may God give you pardon and peace,
and I absolve you from your sins**

**in the name of the Father, and of the Son, ✠
and of the Holy Spirit.**

The penitent answers: **Amen.**

PROCLAMATION OF PRAISE FOR GOD'S MERCY

56. When the individual confessions have been completed,
the other priests stand near the one who is presiding over
the celebration. The latter invites all present to offer thanks
and encourages them to do good works which will proclaim
the grace of repentance in the life of the entire community
and each of its members. It is fitting for all to sing a psalm or
hymn or to say a litany in acknowledgment of God's power
and mercy, for example, the canticle of Mary (Luke 1:46-55),
or Psalm 135:1-9, 13-14, 16, 25-26.

CANTICLE OF MARY (MAGNIFICAT)

**My soul proclaims the greatness of the Lord,
my spirit rejoices in God my Savior
for he has looked with favor on his lowly servant.**

**From this day all generations will call me blessed:
the Almighty has done great things for me,
and holy is his Name.**

**He has mercy on those who fear him
in every generation.**

**He has shown the strength of his arm,
he has scattered the proud in their conceit.**

**He has cast down the mighty from their thrones,
and has lifted up the lowly.**

**He has filled the hungry with good things,
and the rich he has sent away empty.**

**He has come to the help of his servant Israel
for he has remembered his promise of mercy,
the promise he made to our fathers,
to Abraham and his children for ever.**

Psalm 135:1-9, 13-14, 16, 25-26

Alleluia!
O give thanks to the Lord for he is good,
for his love endures for ever.
Give thanks to the God of gods,
for his love endures for ever.
Give thanks to the Lord of lords,
for his love endures for ever;

who alone has wrought marvellous works,
for his love endures for ever;
whose wisdom it was made the skies,
for his love endures for ever;
who fixed the earth firmly on the seas,
for his love endures for ever.

It was he who made the great lights,
for his love endures for ever,
the sun to rule in the day,
for his love endures for ever,
the moon and stars in the night,
for his love endures for ever.

He divided the Red Sea in two,
for his love endures for ever;
he made Israel pass through the midst,
for his love endures for ever;

Through the desert his people he led,
for his love endures for ever.
He gives food to all living things,
for his love endures for ever.
To the God of heaven give thanks,
for his love endures for ever.

CONCLUDING PRAYER OF THANKSGIVING

57. After the song of praise or the litany, the priest concludes the common prayer:

Almighty and merciful God,
how wonderfully you created man
and still more wonderfully remade him.
You do not abandon the sinner
but seek him out with a father's love.
You sent your Son into the world
to destroy sin and death
by his passion,
and to restore life and joy
by his resurrection.
You sent the Holy Spirit into our hearts
to make us your children
and heirs of your kingdom.
You constantly renew our spirit
in the sacraments of your redeeming love,
freeing us from slavery to sin
and transforming us ever more closely
into the likeness of your beloved Son.
We thank you for the wonders of your mercy,
and with heart and hand and voice
we join with the whole Church
in a new song of praise:
Glory to you
through Christ
in the Holy Spirit,
now and for ever.
℟. Amen.

Or:
All-holy Father,
you have shown us your mercy
and made us a new creation
in the likeness of your Son.
Make us living signs of your love
for the whole world to see.

We ask this through Christ our Lord.
℟. Amen.

Or [207]:
Father, all-powerful and ever-living God,
we do well always and everywhere to give you
    thanks.
When you punish us, you show your justice;
when you pardon us, you show your kindness;
yet always your mercy enfolds us.
When you chastise us, you do not wish to condemn
    us;
when you spare us, you give us time to make amends
    for our sins
through Christ our Lord.
R̕. Amen.

Or [208]:
Lord God,
creator and ruler of your kingdom of light,
in your great love for this world
you gave up your only Son
for our salvation.
His cross has redeemed us,
his death has given us life,
his resurrection has raised us to glory.
Through him we ask you
to be always present among your family.
Teach us to be reverent in the presence of your glory;
fill our hearts with faith,
our days with good works,
our lives with your love;
may your truth be on our lips
and your wisdom in all our actions,
that we may receive the reward of everlasting life.
We ask this through Christ our Lord.
R̕. Amen.

Or [209]:
Lord Jesus Christ,
your loving forgiveness knows no limits.
You took our human nature
to give us an example of humility
and to make us faithful in every trial.

May we never lose the gifts you have given us,
but if we fall into sin,
lift us up by your gift of repentance,
for you live and reign for ever and ever.
R̶. **Amen.**

Or [210]:
Father,
in your love you have brought us
from evil to good and from misery to happiness.
Through your blessings
give the courage of perseverance
to those you have called and justified by faith.

Grant this through Christ our Lord.
R̶. **Amen.**

Or [211]:
God and Father of us all,
you have forgiven our sins
and sent us your peace.
Help us to forgive each other
and to work together to establish peace in the world.

We ask this through Christ our Lord.
R̶. **Amen.**

CONCLUDING RITE

58. Then the priest blesses all present:

May the Lord guide your hearts in the way of his love
and fill you with Christ-like patience.
R̶. **Amen.**

May he give you strength
to walk in newness of life
and to please him in all things.
R̶. **Amen.**

May almighty God bless you,
the Father, and the Son, ✠ and the Holy Spirit.
R̶. **Amen.**

Or [212]:
**And may the blessing of almighty God,
the Father, and the Son, + and the Holy Spirit,
come upon you and remain with you for ever.**
R̸. **Amen.**

Or [213]:
**May the Father bless us,
for we are his children, born to eternal life.**
R̸. **Amen.**

**May the Son show us his saving power,
for he died and rose for us.**
R̸. **Amen.**

**May the Spirit give us his gift of holiness
and lead us by the right path,
for he dwells in our hearts.**
R̸. **Amen.**

Or [214]:
**May the Father bless us,
for he has adopted us as his children.**
R̸. **Amen.**

**May the Son come to help us,
for he has received us as brothers and sisters.**
R̸. **Amen.**

**May the Spirit be with us,
for he has made us his dwelling place.**
R̸. **Amen.**

59. The deacon or other minister or the priest himself
dismisses the assembly:

The Lord has freed you from your sins. Go in peace.
All answer: **Thanks be to God.**

Any other appropriate form may be used.

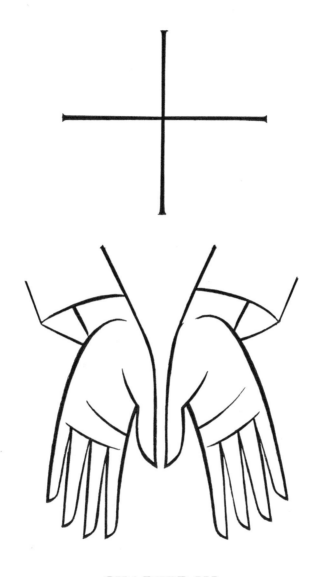

CHAPTER III

RITE FOR RECONCILIATION OF SEVERAL PENITENTS WITH GENERAL CONFESSION AND ABSOLUTION

60. For the reconciliation of several penitents with general confession and absolution, in the cases provided for in the law, everything is done as described above for the reconciliation of several penitents with individual absolution, but with the following changes only.

INSTRUCTION

After the homily or as part of the homily, the priest explains to the faithful who wish to receive general absolution that they should be properly disposed. Each one should repent of his sins and resolve to turn away from these sins, to make up for any scandal and harm he may have caused, and to confess individually at the proper time each of the serious sins which cannot now be confessed. Some form of satisfaction should be proposed to all, and each individual may add something if he desires.

GENERAL CONFESSION

61. Then the deacon or other minister or the priest himself invites the penitents who wish to receive absolution to indicate this by some kind of sign. He may say:

Will those of you who wish to receive sacramental absolution please kneel and acknowledge that you are sinners.

Or:

Will those of you who wish to receive sacramental absolution please bow your heads and acknowledge that you are sinners.

Or he may suggest a sign laid down by the episcopal conference.

The penitents say a general formula for confession (for example, **I confess to almighty God**). A litany or appropriate song may follow, as described above for the reconciliation of several penitents with individual confession and absolution (no. 54). The Lord's Prayer is always added at the end.

GENERAL ABSOLUTION

62. The priest then gives absolution, holding his hands extended over the penitents and saying:

**God the Father does not wish the sinner to die
but to turn back to him and live.
He loved us first and sent his Son into the world to be
its Savior.
May he show you his merciful love and give you
peace.**
R̰. **Amen.**

**Our Lord Jesus Christ was given up to death for our
sins,
and rose again for our justification.
He sent the Holy Spirit on his apostles
and gave them power to forgive sins.
Through the ministry entrusted to me
may he deliver you from evil
and fill you with his Holy Spirit.**
R̰. **Amen.**

**The Spirit, the Comforter, was given to us for the
forgiveness of sins.
In him we approach the Father.
May he cleanse your hearts and clothe you in his
glory,
so that you may proclaim the mighty acts of God
who has called you out of darkness into the splendor
of his light.**
R̰. **Amen.**

**And I absolve you from your sins
in the name of the Father, and of the Son, ✠
and of the Holy Spirit.**
R̰. **Amen.**

Or:
**God, the Father of mercies,
through the death and resurrection of his Son**

has reconciled the world to himself
and sent the Holy Spirit among us
for the forgiveness of sins;
through the ministry of the Church
may God give you pardon and peace,
and I absolve you from your sins
in the name of the Father, and of the Son, ✠
and of the Holy Spirit.
℟. Amen.

PROCLAMATION OF PRAISE AND CONCLUSION

63. The priest invites all to thank God and to acknowledge
his mercy. After a suitable song or hymn, he blesses the
people and dismisses them, as described above, nos. 58-59,
but without the concluding prayer (no. 57).

SHORT RITE

64. In case of necessity, the rite for reconciling several
penitents with general confession and absolution may be
shortened. If possible, there is a brief reading from
scripture. After giving the usual instruction (no. 60) and
indicating the act of penance, the priest invites the penitents
to make a general confession (for example, **I confess to
almighty God**), and gives the absolution with the form
which is indicated in no. 62.

65. In imminent danger of death, it is enough for the priest
to use the form of absolution itself. In this case it may be
shortened to the following:

**I absolve you from your sins
in the name of the Father, and of the Son, ✠
and of the Holy Spirit.**
℟. **Amen.**

66. A person who receives general absolution from grave
sins is bound to confess each grave sin at his next individual
confession.

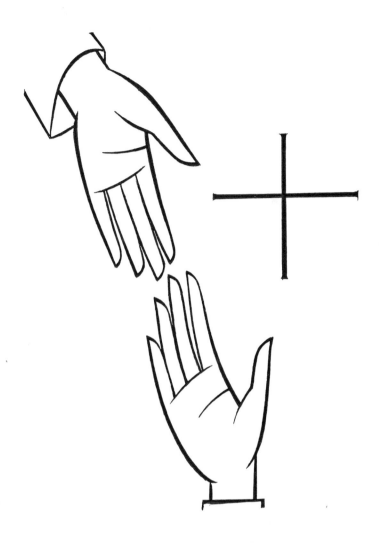

CHAPTER IV

VARIOUS TEXTS USED

IN THE

CELEBRATION OF RECONCILIATION

I. FOR THE RECONCILIATION OF ONE PENITENT

INVITATION TO TRUST IN GOD

67. Ezekiel 33:11

**The Lord does not wish the sinner to die
but to turn back to him and live.
Come before him with trust in his mercy.**

68. Luke 5:32

**May the Lord Jesus welcome you.
He came to call sinners, not the just.
Have confidence in him.**

69.

**May the grace of the Holy Spirit
fill your heart with light,
that you may confess your sins with loving trust
and come to know that God is merciful.**

70.

**May the Lord be in your heart
and help you to confess your sins with true sorrow.**

71. 1 John 2:1-2

**If you have sinned, do not lose heart.
We have Jesus Christ to plead for us with the Father:
he is the Holy One,
the atonement for our sins
and for the sins of the whole world.**

SHORT READINGS FROM SCRIPTURE

**Let us look on Jesus
who suffered to save us
and rose again for our justification.**

72. Isaiah 53:4-6

**Ours were the sufferings he bore,
ours the sorrows he carried.**

But we, we thought of him as someone punished,
struck by God, and brought low.
Yet he was pierced through for our faults,
crushed for our sins.
On him lies a punishment that brings us peace,
and through his wounds we are healed.

We had all gone astray like sheep,
each taking his own way,
and the Lord burdened him
with the sins of all of us.

73. Ezekiel 11:19-20
Let us listen to the Lord as he speaks to us:

I will give them a single heart
   and I will put a new spirit in them;
I will remove the heart of stone from their bodies
   and give them a heart of flesh instead,
      so that they will keep my laws and respect my observances
      and put them into practice.
Then they shall be my people and I will be their God.

74. Matthew 6:14-15
Let us listen to the Lord as he speaks to us:

Yes, if you forgive others their failings,
your heavenly Father will forgive you yours;
but if you do not forgive others,
your Father will not forgive your failings either.

75. Mark 1:14-15
After John had been arrested, Jesus went into Galilee.
There he proclaimed the Good News from God.
"The time has come," he said,
   "and the kingdom of God is close at hand.
Repent, and believe the Good News."

76. Luke 6:31-38
Let us listen to the Lord as he speaks to us:

Treat others as you would like them to treat you.
If you love those who love you,
what thanks can you expect?
Even sinners love those who love them.
And if you do good to those who do good to you,
what thanks can you expect?
For even sinners do that much.
And if you lend to those from whom you hope to receive,
what thanks can you expect?
Even sinners lend to sinners to get back the same amount.
Instead, love your enemies and do good,
and lend without any hope of return.
You will have a great reward,
and you will be sons of the Most High,
for he himself is kind to the ungrateful and the wicked.

Be compassionate as your Father is compassionate.
Do not judge, and you will not be judged yourselves;
do not condemn, and you will not be condemned yourselves;
grant pardon, and you will be pardoned.
Give, and there will be gifts for you:
a full measure, pressed down, shaken together,
and running over, will be poured into your lap;
because the amount you measure out
is the amount you will be given back.

77. Luke 15:1-7

The tax collectors and the sinners were
   all seeking his company to hear what he had to say,
   and the Pharisees and the scribes complained.
"This man," they said, "welcomes sinners and eats with them."
So he spoke this parable to them:

"What man among you with a hundred sheep, losing one,
   would not leave the ninety-nine in the wilderness
   and go after the missing one till he found it?
And when he found it,
   would he not joyfully take it on his shoulders and then,
   when he got home, call together his friends and neighbors?
'Rejoice with me,' he would say,
   'I have found my sheep that was lost.' "

In the same way, I tell you,
  there will be more rejoicing in heaven
  over one repentant sinner than over ninety-nine
  virtuous men who have no need of repentance.

78. John 10:19-23

In the evening of that same day, the first day of the week,
  the doors were closed in the room where the disciples were,
  for fear of the Jews. Jesus came and stood among them.
He said to them, "Peace be with you,"
  and showed them his hands and his side.
The disciples were filled with joy when they saw the Lord,
  and he said to them again, "Peace be with you.
  "As the Father sent me,
  so I am sending you."
After saying this he breathed on them and said:
  "Receive the Holy Spirit.
  For those whose sins you forgive,
  they are forgiven;
  for those whose sins you retain,
  they are retained."

79. Romans 5:8-9

What proves that God loves us is
  that Christ died for us while we were still sinners.
Having died to make us righteous, is it likely
  that he would now fail to save us from God's anger?

80. Ephesians 5:1-2

Try to imitate God, as children of his that he loves,
  and follow Christ by loving as he loved you,
giving himself up in our place
  as a fragrant offering and a sacrifice to God.

81. Colossians 1:12-14

Give thanks to the Father who has made it possible
  for you to join the saints
  and with them to inherit the light.

Because that is what he has done:
  he has taken us out of the power of darkness

and created a place for us
in the kingdom of the Son that he loves,
and in him, we gain our freedom, the forgiveness of our sins.

82. Colossians 3:8-10, 12-17

Now you, of all people, must give all these things up:
   getting angry, being bad-tempered, spitefulness,
   abusive language and dirty talk;
and never tell each other lies.
You have stripped off your old behavior with your old self,
   and you have put on a new self
   which will progress toward true knowledge
   the more it is renewed in the image of its creator.

You are God's chosen race, his saints;
he loves you, and you should be clothed
   in sincere compassion, in kindness and humility,
   gentleness and patience.
Bear with one another;
   forgive each other as soon as a quarrel begins.
The Lord has forgiven you; now you must do the same.
Over all these clothes, to keep them together
   and complete them, put on love.
And may the peace of Christ reign in your hearts,
   because it is for this that you were called together
   as parts of one body.
Always be thankful.

Let the message of Christ, in all its richness,
   find a home with you.
Teach each other, and advise each other, in all wisdom.
With gratitude in your hearts sing psalms and hymns
   and inspired songs to God;
and never say or do anything
   except in the name of the Lord Jesus,
   giving thanks to God the Father through him.

83. 1 John 1:6-7, 9

If we say that we are in union with God
   while we are living in darkness,
   we are lying because we are not living the truth.

But if we live our lives in the light,
  as he is in the light,
  we are in union with one another,
  and the blood of Jesus, his Son,
  purifies us from all sin.
But if we acknowledge our sins,
  then God who is faithful and just
  will forgive our sins and purify us
  from everything that is wrong.

84. A reading may also be chosen from those given in nos. 101-201 for the reconciliation of several penitents. The priest and penitent may choose other readings from scripture.

PRAYER OF THE PENITENT

85. Psalm 24:6-7

Remember, Lord, your compassion and mercy which you
  showed long ago.
Do not recall the sins and failings of my youth.
In your mercy remember me, Lord, because of your
  goodness.

86. Psalm 50:4-5

Wash me from my guilt
and cleanse me of my sin.
I acknowledge my offense;
my sin is before me always.

87. Luke 15:18; 18:13

Father, I have sinned against you
and am not worthy to be called your son.
Be merciful to me, a sinner.

88.

Father of mercy,
like the prodigal son
I return to you and say:
"I have sinned against you
and am no longer worthy to be called your son."
Christ Jesus, Savior of the world,
I pray with the repentant thief
to whom you promised paradise:
"Lord, remember me in your kingdom."

Holy Spirit, fountain of love,
I call on you with trust:
"Purify my heart,
and help me to walk as a child of the light."

89.
Lord Jesus,
you opened the eyes of the blind,
healed the sick,
forgave the sinful woman,
and after Peter's denial confirmed him in your love.
Listen to my prayer:
forgive all my sins,
renew your love in my heart,
help me to live in perfect unity with my fellow
    Christians
that I may proclaim your saving power to all the
    world.

90.
Lord Jesus,
you chose to be called the friend of sinners.
By your saving death and resurrection
free me from my sins.
May your peace take root in my heart
and bring forth a harvest
of love, holiness, and truth.

91.
Lord Jesus Christ,
you are the Lamb of God;
you take away the sins of the world.
Through the grace of the Holy Spirit
restore me to friendship with your Father,
cleanse me from every stain of sin
in the blood you shed for me,
and raise me to new life
for the glory of your name.

92.

**Lord God,
in your goodness have mercy on me:
do not look on my sins,
but take away all my guilt.
Create in me a clean heart
and renew within me an upright spirit.**

Or:

**Lord Jesus, Son of God,
have mercy on me, a sinner.**

AFTER THE ABSOLUTION

93. In place of the proclamation of God's praise and the dismissal, the priest may say:

**May the Passion of our Lord Jesus Christ,
the intercession of the Blessed Virgin Mary and of all
  the saints,
whatever good you do and suffering you endure,
heal your sins,
help you grow in holiness,
and reward you with eternal life.
Go in peace.**

Or:

**The Lord has freed you from sin.
May he bring you safely to his kingdom in heaven.
Glory to him for ever.**
℟. **Amen.**

Or:

**Blessed are those
whose sins have been forgiven,
whose evil deeds have been forgotten.
Rejoice in the Lord,
and go in peace.**

Or:

**Go in peace,
and proclaim to the world**

the wonderful works of God,
who has brought you salvation.

II. FOR THE RECONCILIATION OF SEVERAL PENITENTS

GREETING

94.

Grace, mercy, and peace
from God the Father and Jesus Christ his Son
be with you in truth and love.
℟. **Amen.**

95.

May God open your hearts to his law
and give you peace;
may he answer your prayers
and restore you to his friendship.
℟. **Amen.**

✓ 96.

Grace and peace be with you
from God our Father
and from the Lord Jesus Christ
who laid down his life for our sins.
℟. **Glory to him for ever. Amen.**

The greetings from the introductory rites of Mass may also be used.

OPENING PRAYERS

97.

Lord,
turn to us in mercy
and forgive us all our sins
that we may serve you in true freedom.

We ask this through Christ our Lord.
℟. **Amen.**

98.

Lord our God,
you are patient with sinners

and accept our desire to make amends.
We acknowledge our sins
and are resolved to change our lives.
Help us to celebrate this sacrament of your mercy
so that we may reform our lives
and receive from you the gift of everlasting joy.

We ask this through Christ our Lord.
R̷. **Amen.**

99.
Almighty and merciful God,
you have brought us together in the name of your Son
to receive your mercy and grace in our time of need.
Open our eyes to see the evil we have done.
Touch our hearts and convert us to yourself.

Where sin has divided and scattered,
may your love make one again;
where sin has brought weakness,
may your power heal and strengthen;
where sin has brought death,
may your Spirit raise to new life.

Give us a new heart to love you,
so that our lives may reflect the image of your Son.
May the world see the glory of Christ
revealed in your Church,
and come to know
that he is the one whom you have sent,
Jesus Christ, your Son, our Lord.
R̷. **Amen.**

100.
Father of mercies
and God of all consolation,
you do not wish the sinner to die
but to be converted and live.
Come to the aid of your people,
that they may turn from their sins
and live for you alone.
May we be attentive to your word,
confess our sins, receive your forgiveness,

and be always grateful for your loving kindness.
Help us to live the truth in love
and grow into the fullness of Christ, your Son,
who lives and reigns for ever and ever.
R̷. Amen.

BIBLICAL READINGS

The following readings are proposed as a help for pastors and
others involved in the selection of readings. For diversity, and
according to the nature of the group, other readings may be
selected.

READINGS FROM THE OLD TESTAMENT

101. Genesis 3:1-19   She took the fruit of the tree and ate it.

A reading from the book of Genesis
The serpent was the most subtle of all the wild beasts
    that the Lord God had made.
It asked the woman, "Did God really say
    you were not to eat from any of the trees in the garden?"
The woman answered the serpent,
    "We may eat the fruit of the trees in the garden.
But of the fruit of the tree
    in the middle of the garden God said,
    'You must not eat it, nor touch it, under pain of death.' "
Then the serpent said to the woman, "No! You will not die!
God knows in fact that on the day you eat it
    your eyes will be opened and you will be like gods,
    knowing good and evil."
The woman saw that the tree was good to eat
    and pleasing to the eye,
    and that it was desirable for the knowledge that it could give.
So she took some of its fruit and ate it.
She gave some also to her husband who was with her,
    and he ate it.
Then the eyes of both of them were opened
    and they realized that they were naked.
So they sewed fig-leaves together
    to make themselves loin-cloths.

The man and his wife heard the sound
  of the Lord God walking in the garden in the cool of the day,
  and they hid from the Lord God
  among the trees of the garden.
But the Lord God called to the man.
"Where are you?" he asked.
"I heard the sound of you in the garden,"
  he replied. "I was afraid because I was naked, so I hid."
"Who told you that you were naked?" he asked.
  "Have you been eating of the tree I forbade you to eat?"
The man replied, "It was the woman you put with me;
  she gave me the fruit, and I ate it."
Then the Lord God asked the woman,
  "What is this you have done?"
The woman replied, "The serpent tempted me and I ate."
Then the Lord God said to the serpent,
  "Because you have done this,

  "Be accursed beyond all cattle,
  all wild beasts.
  You shall crawl on your belly and eat dust
  every day of your life.
  I will make you enemies of each other:
  you and the woman,
  your offspring and her offspring.
  It will crush your head
  and you will strike its heel."

To the woman he said:
  "I will multiply your pains in childbearing,
  you shall give birth to your children in pain.
  Your yearning shall be for your husband,
  yet he will lord it over you."

To the man he said, "Because you listened to the voice
  of your wife and ate from the tree
  of which I had forbidden you to eat,

  "Accursed be the soil because of you.
  With suffering shall you get your food from it
  every day of your life.
  It shall yield you brambles and thistles,
  and you shall eat wild plants.
  With sweat on your brow

shall you eat your bread,
until you return to the soil,
as you were taken from it.
For dust you are
and to dust you shall return."
This is the Word of the Lord.

102. Genesis 4:1-15 Cain set on his brother and killed him.

A reading from the book of Genesis
The man had intercourse with his wife Eve,
  and she conceived and gave birth to Cain.
"I have acquired a man with the help of the Lord," she said.
She gave birth to a second child, Abel,
  the brother of Cain.
Now Abel became a shepherd and kept flocks,
  while Cain tilled the soil.
Time passed and Cain brought some of the produce
  of the soil as an offering for the Lord,
  while Abel for his part brought the first-born of his flock
  and some of their fat as well.
The Lord looked with favor on Abel and his offering.
But he did not look with favor on Cain and his offering,
  and Cain was very angry and downcast.
The Lord asked Cain, "Why are you angry and downcast?
If you are well disposed,
  ought you not to lift up your head?
But if you are ill disposed, is not sin at the door
  like a crouching beast hungering for you,
  which you must master?"
Cain said to his brother Abel, "Let us go out";
  and while they were in the open country,
  Cain set on his brother Abel and killed him.
The Lord asked Cain, "Where is your brother Abel?"
"I do not know," he replied. "Am I my brother's guardian?"
"What have you done?" the Lord asked.
"Listen to the sound of your brother's blood,
  crying out to me from the ground.
Now be accursed and driven from the ground
  that has opened its mouth
  to receive your brother's blood at your hands.
When you till the ground
  it shall no longer yield you any of its produce.

You shall be a fugitive and a wanderer over the earth."
Then Cain said to the Lord,
   "My punishment is greater than I can bear.
See! Today you drive me from this ground.
I must hide from you,
   and be a fugitive and a wanderer over the earth.
Why, whoever comes across me will kill me!"
"Very well, then," the Lord replied,
   "if anyone kills Cain,
   sevenfold vengeance shall be taken for him."
So the Lord put a mark on Cain, to prevent whoever
   might come across him from striking him down.
   This is the Word of the Lord.

103. Genesis 18:17-33   The Lord said: I will not destroy the
city for the sake of ten good men.

A reading from the book of Genesis
Now the Lord had wondered,
   "Shall I conceal from Abraham what I am going to do,
   seeing that Abraham will become a great nation
   with all the nations of the earth blessing themselves by him?
For I have singled him out to command his sons
   and his household after him to maintain the way of the Lord
   by just and upright living.
In this way the Lord will carry out for Abraham
   what he has promised him."
Then the Lord said,
   "How great an outcry there is against Sodom and Gomorrah!
How grievous is their sin!
I propose to go down and see
   whether or not they have done all that is alleged
   in the outcry against them that has come up to me.
I am determined to know."

The men left there and went to Sodom
   while Abraham remained standing before the Lord.
Approaching him he said,
   "Are you really going to destroy the just man with the sinner?
Perhaps there are fifty just men in the town.
Will you really overwhelm them,
   will you not spare the place for the fifty just men in it?
Do not think of doing such a thing:

to kill the just man with the sinner,
treating just and sinner alike!
Do not think of it!
Will the judge of the whole earth not administer justice?"
The Lord replied,
"If at Sodom I find fifty just men in the town,
I will spare the whole place because of them."

Abraham replied,
"I am bold indeed to speak like this to my Lord,
I who am dust and ashes.
But perhaps the fifty just men lack five:
will you destroy a whole city for five?"
"No," he replied
"I will not destroy it if I find forty-five just men there."
Again Abraham said to him,
"Perhaps there will only be forty there."
"I will not do it," he replied, "for the sake of forty."

Abraham said,
"I trust my Lord will not be angry,
but give me leave to speak:
perhaps there will only be thirty there."
"I will not do it," he replied, "if I find thirty there."
He said, "I am bold indeed to speak of this,
but perhaps there will only be twenty there."
"I will not destroy it," he replied, "for the sake of the twenty."
He said,
"I trust my Lord will not be angry if I speak once more:
perhaps there will only be ten."
"I will not destroy it," he replied, "for the sake of the ten."

When he had finished talking to Abraham the Lord went away,
and Abraham returned home.
This is the Word of the Lord.

104. Exodus 17:1-7   They tempted the Lord saying: Is the
Lord here or not?

A reading from the book of Exodus
The whole community of the sons of Israel
moved from their camp in the wilderness of Sin
at the Lord's command, to travel the further stages;
and they pitched camp at Rephidim
where there was no water for the people to drink.

So they grumbled against Moses.
"Give us water to drink," they said.
Moses answered them. "Why do you grumble against me?
Why do you put the Lord to the test?"
But tormented by thirst, the people complained against Moses.
"Why did you bring us out of Egypt?" they said,
    "Was it so that I should die of thirst,
    my children too, and my cattle?" Moses appealed to the Lord.
"How am I to deal with this people?" he said.
"A little more and they will stone me!"
The Lord said to Moses, "Take with you some of the elders
    of Israel and move on to the forefront of the people;
    take in your hand the staff with which you struck the river,
    and go.
I shall be standing before you there on the rock,
    at Horeb. You must strike the rock,
    and water will flow from it for the people to drink."
This is what Moses did, in the sight of the elders of Israel.
The place was named Massah and Meribah
    because of the grumbling of the sons of Israel
    and because they put the Lord to the test by saying,
    "Is the Lord with us, or not?"
This is the Word of the Lord.

105. Exodus 20:1-21   I am the Lord your God . . . you will not
have other gods.

A reading from the book of Exodus
Then God spoke all these words.
He said, "I am the Lord your God who brought you
    out of the land of Egypt, out of the house of slavery.

"You shall have no gods except me.

"You shall not make yourself a carved image
    or any likeness of anything in heaven
    or on earth beneath or in the waters under the earth;
    you shall not bow down to them or serve them.
For I, the Lord your God, am a jealous God
    and I punish the father's fault in the sons, the grandsons,
    and the great-grandsons of those who hate me;
    but I show kindness to thousands of those who love me
    and keep my commandments.

"You shall not utter the name of the Lord your God to misuse it,

for the Lord will not leave unpunished
the man who utters his name to misuse it.

"Remember the sabbath day and keep it holy.
For six days you shall labor and do all your work,
  but the seventh day is a sabbath for the Lord your God.
You shall do no work that day,
  neither you nor your son nor your daughter
  nor your servants, men or women,
  nor your animals nor the stranger who lives with you.
For in six days the Lord made the heavens and the earth
  and the sea and all that these hold,
  but on the seventh day he rested;
  that is why the Lord has blessed the sabbath day
  and made it sacred.

"Honor your father and your mother
  so that you may have a long life in the land
  that the Lord your God has given to you.
  You shall not kill.
  You shall not commit adultery.
  You shall not steal.
  You shall not bear false witness against your neighbor.
  You shall not covet your neighbor's house.
  You shall not covet your neighbor's wife, or his servant,
  man or woman, or his ox, or his donkey, or anything that is his."

All the people shook with fear at the peals of thunder
  and the lightning flashes, the sound of the trumpet,
  and the smoking mountain; and they kept their distance.
"Speak to us yourself," they said to Moses, "and we will listen;
  but do not let God speak to us, or we shall die."
Moses answered the people, "Do not be afraid;
  God has come to test you, so that your fear of him,
  being always in your mind, may keep you from sinning."
So the people kept their distance
  while Moses approached the dark cloud where God was.
  This is the Word of the Lord.

106. Deuteronomy 6:3-9   Love the Lord your God with your
whole heart

A reading from the book of Deuteronomy
"Listen then, Israel,
  keep and observe what will make you prosper

and give you great increase,
as the Lord the God of your fathers has promised you,
giving you a land where milk and honey flow.

"Listen Israel: the Lord our God is the one Lord.
You shall love the Lord your God with all your heart,
with all your soul, with all your strength.
Let these words I urge on you today
be written on your heart.
You shall repeat them to your children
and say them over to them whether at rest in your house
or walking abroad, at your lying down or at your rising;
you shall fasten them on your hand as a sign
and on your forehead as a circlet;
you shall write them on the doorposts of your house
and on your gates."
This is the Word of the Lord.

107. Deuteronomy 9:7-19   Your people quickly turned away
from the wrong you had showed them.

A reading from the book of Deuteronomy
"Remember;
never forget how you provoked
the Lord your God in the wilderness.
from the day you came out of the land of Egypt
you have been rebels against the Lord.
At Horeb you provoked the Lord,
and the Lord was so angry with you
that he was ready to destroy you.
I had gone up the mountain to receive the tablets of stone,
the tablets of the covenant
that the Lord was making with you.
I stayed forty days and forty nights on the mountain,
eating no bread, drinking no water.
The Lord gave me the two stone tablets
inscribed by the finger of God,
and all the words on them that the Lord had spoken to you
on the mountain from the midst of the fire
on the day of the Assembly.
At the end of the forty days and forty nights,
after he had given me the two tablets of stone,
the tablets of the covenant,
the Lord said to me,

'Leave this place, go down quickly, for your people
　whom you brought out of Egypt have broken faith.
They have been quick to leave the way I marked out for them;
　they have made themselves an idol of cast metal.'
Then the Lord said to me,
　'I have seen this people,
　and what a headstrong people they are!
Let me destroy them,
　and wipe out their name from under heaven,
　and make out of you a nation
　mightier and greater than they.'

"So I went down the mountain again
　and it was blazing with fire,
　and in my hands were the two tablets of the covenant.
And I looked and there you were,
　you had been sinning against the Lord your God.
You had made yourself a calf of cast metal;
　you had been quick to leave the way
　the Lord marked out for you.
I seized the two tablets
　and with my two hands threw them down
　and broke them before your eyes.
Then I fell prostrate before the Lord;
　as before, I passed forty days and forty nights
　eating no bread and drinking no water,
　for all the sin you had committed
　in doing what was displeasing to the Lord,
　thus arousing his anger.
For I was afraid of this anger, of the fury
　which so roused the Lord against you
　that he was ready to destroy you.
And once more the Lord heard my prayer."
This is the Word of the Lord.

108. Deuteronomy 30:15-20   I set before you life and prosperity, death and evil.

A reading from the book of Deuteronomy
"See,
　today I set before you life and prosperity, death and disaster.
If you obey the commandments of the Lord your God
　that I enjoin on you today,

if you love the Lord your God and follow his ways,
if you keep his commandments, his laws, his customs,
you will live and increase,
and the Lord your God will bless you in the land
which you are entering to make your own.
But if your heart strays, if you refuse to listen,
if you let yourself be drawn into worshiping other gods
and serving them,
I tell you today, you will most certainly perish;
you will not live long in the land
you are crossing the Jordan to enter and possess.
I call heaven and earth to witness against you today:
I set before you life or death, blessing or curse.
Choose life, then, so that you and your descendants may live,
in the love of the Lord your God,
obeying his voice, clinging to him;
for in this your life consists, and on this depends
your long stay in the land which the Lord swore
to your fathers Abraham, Isaac and Jacob he would give them."
This is the Word of the Lord.

109. 2 Samuel 12:1-9, 13   David said to Nathan: I have sinned
against the Lord God. Nathan said to David: The Lord has
forgiven your sin; you will not die.

A reading from the Second Book of Samuel
The Lord sent Nathan the prophet to David.
He came to him and said:

"In the same town were two men,
one rich, the other poor.
The rich man had flocks and herds
in great abundance;
the poor man had nothing but a ewe lamb,
one only, a small one he had bought.
This he fed, and it grew up with him and his children,
eating his bread, drinking from his cup,
sleeping on his breast; it was like a daughter to him.
When there came a traveler to stay, the rich man
refused to take one of his own flock or herd
to provide for the wayfarer who had come to him.
Instead he took the poor man's lamb
and prepared it for his guest."

David's anger flared up against the man.
"As the Lord lives," he said to Nathan
   "the man who did this deserves to die!
He must make fourfold restitution for the lamb,
   for doing such a thing and showing no compassion."

Then Nathan said to David, "You are the man.
The Lord the God of Israel says this,
   'I anointed you king over Israel;
   I delivered you from the hands of Saul;
   I gave your master's house to you, his wives into your arms;
   I gave you the House of Israel and of Judah;
   and if this were not enough,
   I would add as much again for you.
Why have you shown contempt for the Lord,
   doing what displeases him?
You have struck down Uriah the Hittite with the sword,
   taken his wife for your own,
   and killed him with the sword of the Ammonites.' "

David said to Nathan, "I have sinned against the Lord."
Then Nathan said to David,
   "The Lord, for his part, forgives your sin;
   you are not to die."
This is the Word of the Lord.

110. Nehemiah 9:1-20   The sons of Israel assembled for a fast
and confessed their sins.

A reading from the book of the prophet Nehemiah
On the twenty-fourth day of this month the Israelites,
   in sackcloth and with dust on their heads,
   assembled for a fast.
Those of Israelite stock separated themselves
   from all those of foreign origin;
   they stood confessing their sins
   and the transgressions of their ancestors.
(Standing, each man in his right position,
   they read from the Book of the Law of the Lord their God
   for one quarter of the day;
   for another quarter they confessed their sins
   and prostrated themselves before the Lord their God.)
(On the Levites' platform stood Jeshua, Binnui, Kadmiel,

Shebaniah, Bunni, Sherebiah, Bani and Chenani,
calling loudly to the Lord their God;
and the Levites, Jeshua, Kadmiel, Bani, Hashabneiah,
Sherebiah, Hodiah, Shebaniah and Pethahiah said,
"Arise and bless the Lord our God.")

Blessed be you, the Lord our God,
from everlasting to everlasting.
And blessed be your name of glory
that surpasses all blessing and praise.

Lord, you are the only one.
You made the heavens,
the heaven of heavens, with all their array,
the earth and all it bears,
the seas and all they hold.
To all of these you give life
and the array of the heavens bows down before you.

Lord, you are the God
who chose Abram,
brought him out from Ur in Chaldaea,
and gave him the name of Abraham.
Finding him faithful of heart before you,
you made a covenant with him,
to give him the land of the Canaanite,
of the Hittite and Amorite,
of the Perizzite, Jebusite, Girgashite,
to him and his posterity.
And you kept your promise
because you are just.

You saw the distress of our fathers in Egypt,
you heard their cry by the Sea of Reeds.
You worked portents and miracles against Pharaoh,
against his servants and all the people of his land;
for you knew how they treated them with arrogance.
You won a reputation which you keep to this day.
You divided the sea in front of them:
they passed through the deep sea dry-shod.
Into the depths you hurled their pursuers
like a stone into rushing waters.
With a pillar of cloud you led them by day,
with a pillar of fire by night:

to light the way ahead of them
by which they should go.
You came down on Mount Sinai
and spoke with them from heaven;
you gave them
ordinances that are just,
laws that are sure,
good statutes and commandments;
you taught them to know
your holy sabbath,
laid down for them commandments (statutes) and Law
through Moses your servant.
For their hunger you gave them bread from heaven,
for their thirst you brought them water spurting from the rock.
You bade them go in
and take possession of the land
that you had sworn
to give to them.

But our fathers grew proud,
were obstinate, and flouted your commands.
They refused to obey, forgetful of the wonders
that you had worked for them;
they became obstinate, they even thought
of going back to Egypt and their slavery.
But you are a God of forgiveness,
gracious and loving,
slow to anger, abounding in goodness,
you did not forsake them.

When they cast themselves a calf
out of molten metal
and said, "This is your God
who brought you up from Egypt"
(and were guilty of grave blasphemies),
you, so greatly loving,
still did not forsake them in the wilderness:
the pillar of cloud did not leave them
that led them on their path by day,
nor the pillar of fire by night,
to light the way ahead of them
by which they should go.
You gave them your good spirit

to make them wise,
you did not withhold your manna from their mouths,
you gave them water for their thirst.
This is the Word of the Lord.

111. Wisdom 1:1-16   Love justice, for wisdom will not enter
an evil soul nor live in a body subjected to sin.

A reading from the book of Wisdom
Love virtue, you who are judges on earth,
let honesty prompt your thinking about the Lord,
seek him in simplicity of heart;
since he is to be found
by those who do not put him to the test,
he shows himself to those who do not distrust him.
But selfish intentions divorce from God;
and Omnipotence, put to the test, confounds the foolish.
No, Wisdom will never make its way into a crafty soul
nor stay in a body that is in debt to sin;
the holy spirit of instruction shuns deceit,
it stands aloof from reckless purposes,
is taken aback when iniquity appears.

Wisdom is a spirit, a friend to man,
though she will not pardon the words of a blasphemer,
since God sees into the innermost parts of him,
truly observes his heart,
and listens to his tongue.
The spirit of the Lord, indeed, fills the whole world,
and that which holds all things together
knows every word that is said.
The man who gives voice to injustice
will never go unnoticed,
nor shall avenging Justice pass him by.
For the godless man's deliberations will be examined,
and a report of his words will reach the Lord
to convict him of his crimes.
There is a jealous ear that overhears everything,
not so much as a murmur of complaint escapes it.
Beware, then, of complaining about nothing,
and keep your tongue from finding fault;
since the most secret word will have repercussions,
and a lying mouth deals death to the soul.

Do not court death by the errors of your ways,
nor invite destruction through your own actions.
Death was not God's doing,
he takes no pleasure in the extinction of the living.
To be—for this he created all;
the world's created things have health in them,
in them no fatal poison can be found,
and Hades holds no power on earth;
for virtue is undying.

But the godless call with deed and word for Death,
counting him friend, they wear themselves out for him,
with him they make a pact,
and are fit to be his partners.
This is the Word of the Lord.

112. Wisdom 5:1-16 The hope of the wicked is like down
flying on the wind. The just, however, live for ever.

A reading from the book of Wisdom
Then the virtuous man stands up boldly
to face those who have oppressed him,
those who thought so little of his sufferings.
And they, at the sight of him, will shake with cowards' fear,
amazed he should be saved so unexpectedly.
Stricken with remorse, each will say to the other,
say with a groan and in distress of spirit:

"This is the man we used to laugh at once,
a butt for our sarcasm, fools that we were!
His life we regarded as madness,
his ending as without honor.
How has he come to be counted as one of the sons of God?
How does he come to be assigned a place among the saints?
Clearly we have strayed from the way of truth;
the light of justice has not shone for us,
the sun never rose on us.
We have left no path of lawlessness or ruin unexplored,
we have crossed deserts where there was no track,
but the way of the Lord is one we have never known.
Arrogance, what advantage has this brought us?
Wealth and boasting, what have these conferred on us?
All those things have passed like a shadow,

passed like a fleeting rumor.
Like a ship that cuts through heaving waves—
leaving no trace to show where it has passed,
no wake from its keel in the waves.
Or like a bird flying through the air—
leaving no proof of its passing;
it whips the light air with the stroke of its pinions,
tears it apart in its whirring rush,
drives its way onward with sweeping wing,
and afterwards no sign is seen of its passage.
Or like an arrow shot at a mark,
the pierced air closing so quickly on itself,
there is no knowing which way the arrow has passed.
So with us: scarcely born, we have ceased to be;
of virtue not a trace have we to show,
we have spent ourselves on wickedness instead.

Yes, the hope of the godless is like chaff carried on the wind,
like fine spray driven by the gale;
it disperses like smoke before the wind,
goes like the memory of a one-day guest.

But the virtuous live for ever,
their recompense lies with the Lord,
the Most High takes care of them.
So they shall receive the royal crown of splendor,
the diadem of beauty from the hand of the Lord;
for he will shelter them with his right hand
and shield them with his arm.
This is the Word of the Lord.

113. Sirach 28:1-7   Forgive your neighbor when he hurts you,
and then your sins will be forgiven when you pray.

A reading from the book of Sirach
He who exacts vengeance
    will experience the vengeance of the Lord,
    who keeps strict account of sin.
Forgive your neighbor the hurt he does you,
    and when you pray, your sins will be forgiven.
If a man nurses anger against another,
    can he then demand compassion from the Lord?
Showing no pity for a man like himself,
    can he then plead for his own sins?

Mere creature of flesh, he cherishes resentment;
  who will forgive him his sins?
Remember the last things, and stop hating,
  remember dissolution and death,
  and live by the commandments.
  This is the Word of the Lord.

114. Isaiah 1:2-6, 15-18   I have nourished and educated sons;
however they have rebelled against me.

A reading from the book of the prophet Isaiah
  Listen, you heavens; earth, attend
  for the Lord is speaking,
  "I reared sons, I brought them up,
  but they have rebelled against me.
  The ox knows its owner
  and the ass its master's crib,
  Israel knows nothing,
  my people understands nothing."

  A sinful nation, a people weighed down with guilt,
  a breed of wrong-doers, perverted sons.
  They have abandoned the Lord,
  despised the Holy One of Israel,
  they have turned away from him.

  "Where shall I strike you next,
  since you heap one betrayal on another?
  The whole head is sick, the whole heart grown faint;
  from the sole of the foot to the head there is not a sound spot:
  wounds, bruises, open sores
  not dressed, not bandaged,
  not soothed with oil.

  "When you stretch out your hands
  I turn my eyes away.
  You may multiply your prayers,
  I shall not listen.
  Your hands are covered with blood,
  wash, make yourselves clean.

  "Take your wrong-doing out of my sight.
  Cease to do evil.
  Learn to do good,

search for justice,
help the oppressed,
be just to the orphan,
plead for the widow.

"Come now, let us talk this over,"
says the Lord.
"Though your sins are like scarlet,
they shall be as white as snow;
though they are red as crimson,
they shall be like wool."
This is the Word of the Lord.

115. Isaiah 5:1-7 The vineyard became my delight. He looked
for grapes, but it yielded wild grapes.

A reading from the book of the prophet Isaiah
Let me sing to my friend
the song of his love for his vineyard.

My friend had a vineyard
on a fertile hillside.
He dug the soil, cleared it of stones,
and planted choice vines in it.

In the middle he built a tower,
he dug a press there too.
He expected it to yield grapes,
but sour grapes were all that it gave.

And now, inhabitants of Jerusalem
and men of Judah,
I ask you to judge
between my vineyard and me.
What could I have done for my vineyard
that I have not done?
I expected it to yield grapes.
Why did it yield sour grapes instead?

Very well, I will tell you
what I am going to do to my vineyard:
I will take away its hedge for it to be grazed on,
and knock down its wall for it to be trampled on.
I will lay it waste, unpruned, undug;
overgrown by the briar and the thorn.

I will command the clouds
to rain no rain on it.
Yes, the vineyard of the Lord Sabaoth
is the House of Israel,
and the men of Judah
that chosen plant.
He expected justice, but found bloodshed,
integrity, but only a cry of distress.
This is the Word of the Lord.

116. Isaiah 43:22-28   On account of me your iniquities are blotted out.

A reading from the book of the prophet Isaiah
Jacob, you have not invoked me,
you have not troubled yourself, Israel, on my behalf.
You have not brought me your sheep for holocausts,
nor honored me with sacrifices.
I have never burdened you with oblations,
nor troubled you for incense.
You have spent no money on fragrant cane for me,
you have not filled me with the fat of your sacrifices.
Instead you have burdened me with your sins,
troubled me with your iniquities.
I it is, I it is, who must blot out everything
and not remember your sins.

Cast your mind back, let us judge this together;
state your own case and prove your innocence.
Your first father sinned,
your mediators have rebelled against me.
Your princes have profaned my sanctuary.
So I have handed Jacob over to the ban,
and Israel to insults.
This is the Word of the Lord.

117. Isaiah 53:1-12   The Lord laid upon him our guilt.

A reading from the book of the prophet Isaiah
"Who could believe that we have heard,
and to whom has the power of the Lord been revealed?"
Like a sapling he grew up in front of us,
like a root in arid ground.

Without beauty, without majesty (we saw him),
no looks to attract our eyes;
a thing despised and rejected by men,
a man of sorrows and familiar with suffering,
a man to make people screen their faces;
he was despised and we took no account of him.

And yet ours were the sufferings he bore,
ours the sorrows he carried.
But we, we thought of him as someone punished,
struck by God, and brought low.
Yet he was pierced through for our faults,
crushed for our sins.
On him lies a punishment that brings us peace,
and through his wounds we are healed.

We had all gone astray like sheep,
each taking his own way,
and the Lord burdened him
with the sins of all of us.
Harshly dealt with, he bore it humbly,
he never opened his mouth,
like a lamb that is led to the slaughter-house,
like a sheep that is dumb before its shearers
never opening its mouth.

By force and by law he was taken;
would anyone plead his cause?
Yes, he was torn away from the land of the living;
for our faults struck down in death.
They gave him a grave with the wicked,
a tomb with the rich,
though he had done no wrong
and there had been no perjury in his mouth.
The Lord has been pleased to crush him with suffering.
If he offers his life in atonement,
he shall see his heirs, he shall have a long life
and through him what the Lord wishes will be done.

His soul's anguish over
he shall see the light and be content.
By his sufferings shall my servant justify many,
taking their faults on himself.

Hence I will grant whole hordes for his tribute,
he shall divide the spoil with the mighty,

for surrendering himself to death
and letting himself be taken for a sinner,
while he was bearing the faults of many
and praying all the time for sinners.
This is the Word of the Lord.

✓ 118. Isaiah 55:1-11   Let the wicked man forsake his way and
return to the Lord, and he will have mercy on him because he
is generous in forgiving.

A reading from the book of the prophet Isaiah
Oh, come to the water all you who are thirsty;
though you have no money, come!
Buy corn without money and eat,
and, at no cost, wine and milk.
Why spend money on what is not bread,
your wages on what fails to satisfy?
Listen, listen to me, and you will have good things to eat
and rich food to enjoy.
Pay attention, come to me;
listen, and your soul will live.

With you I will make an everlasting covenant
out of the favors promised to David.
See, I have made of you a witness to the peoples,
a leader and a master of the nations.
See, you will summon a nation you never knew,
those unknown will come hurrying to you,
for the sake of the Lord your God,
of the Holy One of Israel who will glorify you.

Seek the Lord while he is still to be found,
call to him while he is still near.
Let the wicked man abandon his way,
the evil man his thoughts.
Let him turn back to the Lord who will take pity on him,
to our God who is rich in forgiving;
for my thoughts are not your thoughts,
my ways not your ways—it is the Lord who speaks.
Yes, the heavens are as high above earth
as my ways are above your ways,
my thoughts above your thoughts.

Yes, as the rain and the snow come down from the heavens

and do not return without watering the earth,
making it yield and giving growth
to provide seed for the sower and bread for the eating,
so the word that goes from my mouth
does not return to me empty,
without carrying out my will
and succeeding in what it was sent to do.
This is the Word of the Lord.

119. Isaiah 58:1-11   When you give your soul to the hungry
and fulfill the troubled soul, your light will rise like dawn from
the darkness, and your darkness will be like midday.

A reading from the book of the prophet Isaiah
   Shout for all you are worth,
   raise your voice like a trumpet.
   Proclaim their faults to my people,
   their sins to the House of Jacob.

   They seek me day after day,
   they long to know my ways,
   like a nation that wants to act with integrity
   and not ignore the law of its God.

   They ask me for laws that are just,
   they long for God to draw near:
   "Why should we fast if you never see it,
   why do penance if you never notice?"

   Look, you do business on your fastdays,
   you oppress all your workmen;
   look, you quarrel and squabble when you fast
   and strike the poor man with your fist.

   Fasting like yours today
   will never make your voice heard on high.
   Is that the sort of fast that pleases me,
   a truly penitential day for men?

   Hanging your head like a reed,
   lying down on sackcloth and ashes?
   Is that what you call fasting,
   a day acceptable to the Lord?

Is not this the sort of fast that pleases me
—it is the Lord God who speaks—
to break unjust fetters
and undo the thongs of the yoke,

to let the oppressed go free,
and break every yoke,
to share your bread with the hungry,
and shelter the homeless poor,

to clothe the man you see to be naked
and not turn from your own kin?
Then will your light shine like the dawn
and your wound be quickly healed over.

Your integrity will go before you
and the glory of the Lord behind you.
Cry, and the Lord will answer;
call, and he will say, "I am here".

If you do away with the yoke,
the clenched fist, the wicked word,
if you give your bread to the hungry,
and relief to the oppressed,

your light will rise in the darkness,
and your shadows become like noon.
The Lord will always guide you,
giving you relief in desert places.

He will give strength to your bones
and you shall be like a watered garden,
like a spring of water
whose waters never run dry.
This is the Word of the Lord.

120. Isaiah 59:1-4, 9-15   Your iniquities divide you and your
God.

A reading from the book of the prophet Isaiah
    No, the hand of the Lord is not too short to save,
    nor his ear too dull to hear.
    But your iniquities have made a gulf

between you and your God.
Your sins have made him veil his face
so as not to hear you,
since your hands are stained with blood,
your fingers with crime,
your lips utter lies,
your tongues murmur treachery.
No one makes just accusations
or pleads sincerely.
All rely on nothingness, utter falsehood,
conceive harm and give birth to misery.

So justice is removed far away from us,
and integrity keeps its distance.
We looked for light and all is darkness,
for brightness and we walk in the dark.
Like the blind we feel our way along walls
and hesitate like men without eyes.
We stumble as though noon were twilight
and dwell in the dark like the dead.
We growl, all of us, like bears,
and moan like doves,
waiting for the justice that never comes,
for salvation that is removed far away from us.

For our faults in your sight have been many
and our sins are a witness against us.
And indeed our faults are present to our minds,
and we know our iniquities:
rebellion and denial of the Lord,
turning our back on our God,
talking treachery and revolt,
murmuring lies in our heart.
Justice is withheld
and integrity stands aloof;
in the public square sincerity is brought to its knees
and uprightness forbidden to enter.

Sincerity is missing
and he who avoids evil is robbed.
The Lord has seen this, and is indignant
that there is no justice to be seen.
This is the Word of the Lord.

121. Jeremiah 2:1-13   My people have done two evils: they
have abandoned me, the fountain of living water, and have
dug for themselves broken cisterns which hold no water.

A reading from the book of the prophet Jeremiah
The Lord says this:
"I remember the affection of your youth,
the love of your bridal days:
you followed me through the wilderness,
through a land unsown.
Israel was sacred to the Lord;
the first-fruits of his harvest;
anyone who ate of this had to pay for it,
misfortune came to them—
it is the Lord who speaks."
Listen to the word of the Lord, House of Jacob,
and all you families of the House of Israel.
Thus says the Lord,
"What shortcoming did your fathers find in me
that led them to desert me?
Vanity they pursued,
vanity they became.
They never said, 'Where is the Lord,
who brought us out of the land of Egypt
and led us through the wilderness,
through a land arid and scored,
a land of drought and darkness,
a land where no one passes,
and no man lives?'
I brought you to a fertile country
to enjoy its produce and good things;
but no sooner had you entered than you defiled my land,
and made my heritage detestable.
The priests have never asked, 'Where is the Lord?'
Those who administer the Law have no knowledge of me.
The shepherds have rebelled against me;
the prophets have prophesied in the name of Baal,
following things with no power in them.
So I must put you on trial once more
—it is the Lord who speaks—
and your children's children too.
Now take ship for the islands of Kittim
or send to Kedar to enquire.

Take careful notice and observe
if anything like this has happened.
Does a nation change its gods?
—and these are not gods at all!
Yet my people have exchanged their Glory
for what has no power in it.
You heavens, stand aghast at this,
stand stupefied, stand utterly appalled
—it is the Lord who speaks.
Since my people have committed a double crime:
they have abandoned me,
the fountain of living water,
only to dig cisterns for themselves,
leaky cisterns
that hold no water."
This is the Word of the Lord.

122. Jeremiah 7:21-26   Listen to my voice, and I will be your
God, and you will be my people.

A reading from the book of the prophet Jeremiah
The Lord Sabaoth, the God of Israel, says this:
   "Add your holocausts to your sacrifices and eat all the meat.
For when I brought your ancestors out of the land of Egypt,
   I said nothing to them, gave them no orders,
   about holocaust and sacrifice.
These were my orders:
   Listen to my voice, then I will be your God
   and you shall be my people.
Follow right to the end the way that I mark out for you,
   and you will prosper.
But they did not listen, they did not pay attention;
   they followed the dictates of their own evil hearts,
   refused to face me, and turned their backs on me.
From the day your ancestors came out of the land of Egypt
   until today, day after day
   I have persistently sent you all my servants the prophets.
But they have not listened to me, have not paid attention;
   they have grown stubborn
   and behaved worse than their ancestors."
This is the Word of the Lord.

123. Ezekiel 11:14-21   I will take the heart of stone from their
bodies, and I will give them a heart of flesh, so that they may
walk according to my laws.

A reading from the book of the prophet Ezekiel
The word of the Lord was then addressed to me as follows,
   "Son of man, your brothers, your kinsmen,
   the whole House of Israel,
   these are told by the citizens of Jerusalem,
   'You have been sent away from the Lord;
   it is to us that the land was given as our domain.'
Say therefore, 'The Lord God says this:
   Yes, I have sent them far away among the nations
   and I have dispersed them to foreign countries;
   and for a while I have been a sanctuary for them
   in the country to which they have gone.'
Then say, 'The Lord God says this:
   I will gather you together from the peoples,
   I will bring you all back from the countries
   where you have been scattered
   and I will give you the land of Israel.
They will come and will purge it of all the horrors
   and the filthy practices.
I will give them a single heart
   and I will put a new spirit in them;
   I will remove the heart of stone from their bodies
   and give them a heart of flesh instead,
   so that they will keep my laws
   and respect my observances and put them into practice.
Then they shall be my people and I will be their God.
But those whose hearts are set on their idols
   and their filthy practices
   I will call to account for their conduct—
   it is the Lord God who speaks.' "
This is the Word of the Lord.

124. Ezekiel 18:20-32   If a wicked man turns away from his
sins, he shall live and not die.

A reading from the book of the prophet Ezekiel
The man who has sinned is the one who must die;
   a son is not to suffer for the sins of his father,

nor a father for the sins of his son.
To the upright man his integrity will be credited,
   to the wicked his wickedness.

But if the wicked man renounces all the sins he has committed,
   respects my laws and is law-abiding and honest,
   he will certainly live; he will not die.
All the sins he committed will be forgotten from then on;
   he shall live because of the integrity he has practiced.
What!
Am I likely to take pleasure in the death of a wicked man—
   it is the Lord God who speaks—
   and not prefer to see him renounce his wickedness and live?
But if the upright man renounces his integrity,
   commits sin, copies the wicked man
   and practices every kind of filth, is he to live?
All the integrity he has practiced
   shall be forgotten from then on;
   but this is because he himself has broken faith
   and committed sin,
   and for this he shall die.
But you object, "What the Lord does is unjust."
Listen, you House of Israel: is what I do unjust?
Is it not what you do that is unjust?
When the upright man renounces his integrity
   to commit sin and dies because of this,
   he dies because of the evil that he himself has committed.
When the sinner renounces sin to become law-abiding
   and honest, he deserves to live.
He has chosen to renounce all his previous sins;
   he shall certainly live; he shall not die.
And yet the House of Israel objects,
   "What the Lord does is unjust."
Is what I do unjust, you House of Israel?
Is it not what you do that is unjust?
House of Israel, in future I mean to judge each of you
   by what he does—is it the Lord God who speaks.
Repent, renounce all your sins, avoid all occasions of sin!
Shake off all the sins you have committed against me,
   and make yourselves a new heart and a new spirit!
Why are you so anxious to die, House of Israel?
I take no pleasure in the death of anyone—

it is the Lord God who speaks. Repent and live!
This is the Word of the Lord.

125. Ezekiel 36:23-28   I shall sprinkle upon you clean water,
put my spirit within you, and make you walk according to my
commands.

A reading from the book of the prophet Ezekiel
I mean to display the holiness of my great name,
    which has been profaned among the nations,
    which you have profaned among them.
And the nations will learn that I am the Lord—
    it is the Lord God who speaks—
    when I display my holiness for your sake before their eyes.
Then I am going to take you from among the nations
    and gather you together from all the foreign countries,
    and bring you home to your own land.
I shall pour clean water over you and you will be cleansed;
    I shall cleanse you of all your defilement and all your idols.
I shall give you a new heart, and put a new spirit in you;
    I shall remove the heart of stone
    from your bodies and give you a heart of flesh instead.
I shall put my spirit in you,
    and make you keep my laws
    and sincerely respect my observances.
You will live in the land which I gave your ancestors.
You shall be my people and I will be your God.
This is the Word of the Lord.

126. Hosea 2:16-25   I will make a covenant for them on that
day.

A reading from the book of the prophet Hosea
    That is why I am going to lure her
    and lead her out into the wilderness
    and speak to her heart.
    I am going to give her back her vineyards,
    and make the Valley of Achor a gateway of hope.
    There she will respond to me as she did when she was young,
    as she did when she came out of the land of Egypt.

    When that day comes—it is the Lord who speaks—

she will call me, "My husband,"
no longer will she call me, "My Baal."
I will take the names of the Baals off her lips,
their names shall never be uttered again.

When that day comes
I will make a treaty on her behalf with the wild animals,
with the birds of heaven and the creeping things of the earth;
I will break bow, sword and battle in the country,
and make her sleep secure.
I will betroth you to myself for ever,
betroth you with integrity and justice,
with tenderness and love;
I will betroth you to myself with faithfulness,
and you will come to know the Lord.

When that day comes—it is the Lord who speaks—
the heavens will have their answer from me,
the earth its answer from them,
the grain, the wine, the oil, their answer from the earth,
and Jezreel his answer from them.
I will sow him in the country,
I will love Unloved;
I will say to No-People-of-Mine, "You are my people,"
and he will answer, "You are my God."
This is the Word of the Lord.

127. Hosea 11:1-11 I took them in my arms, and they did not
know that I cured them.

A reading from the book of the prophet Hosea
    When Israel was a child I loved him,
    and I called my son out of Egypt.
    But the more I called to them, the further they went from me;
    they have offered sacrifice to the Baals
    and set their offerings smoking before the idols.
    I myself taught Ephraim to walk,
    I took them in my arms;
    yet they have not understood
    that I was the one looking after them.
    I led them with reins of kindness,
    with leading-strings of love.
    I was like someone who lifts an infant close against his cheek;

stooping down to him I gave him his food.
They will have to go back to Egypt,
Assyria must be their king,
because they have refused to return to me.
The sword will rage through their towns,
wiping out their children,
glutting itself inside their fortresses.

My people are diseased through their disloyalty;
they call on Baal,
but he does not cure them.
Ephraim, how could I part with you?
Israel, how could I give you up?
How could I treat you like Admah,
or deal with you like Zeboiim?
My heart recoils from it,
my whole being trembles at the thought.
I will not give rein to my fierce anger,
I will not destroy Ephraim again,
for I am God, not man:
I am the Holy One in your midst
and have no wish to destroy.

They will follow behind the Lord;
he will be roaring like a lion—
how he will roar!—
and his sons will come speeding from the west;
they will come speeding from Egypt like a bird,
speeding from the land of Assyria like a dove,
and I will settle them in their homes
—it is the Lord who speaks.
This is the Word of the Lord.

128. Hosea 14:2-10   Israel, return to the Lord your God.

A reading from the book of the prophet Hosea
Israel, come back to the Lord your God;
your iniquity was the cause of your downfall.
Provide yourself with words
and come back to the Lord.
Say to him, "Take all iniquity away
so that we may have happiness again
and offer you our words of praise.

Assyria cannot save us,
we will not ride horses any more,
or say, 'Our God!' to what our own hands have made,
for you are the one in whom orphans find compassion."
—I will heal their disloyalty,
I will love them with all my heart,
for my anger has turned from them.
I will fall like dew on Israel.
He shall bloom like the lily,
and thrust out roots like the poplar,
his shoots will spread far;
he will have the beauty of the olive
and the fragrance of Lebanon.
They will come back to live in my shade;
they will grow corn that flourishes,
they will cultivate vines
as renowned as the wine of Helbon.
What has Ephraim to do with idols any more
when it is I who hear his prayer and care for him?
I am like a cypress ever green,
all your fruitfulness comes from me.

Let the wise man understand these words.
Let the intelligent man grasp their meaning.
For the ways of the Lord are straight,
and virtuous men walk in them,
but sinners stumble.
This is the Word of the Lord.

129. Joel 2:12-19   Return to me with your whole heart.

A reading from the book of the prophet Joel
   "But now, now—it is the Lord who speaks—
   come back to me with all your heart,
   fasting, weeping, mourning."
Let your hearts be broken, not your garments torn,
turn to the Lord your God again,
for he is all tenderness and compassion,
slow to anger, rich in graciousness,
and ready to relent.
Who knows if he will not turn again, will not relent,
will not leave a blessing as he passes,
oblation and libation
for the Lord your God?

Sound the trumpet in Zion!
Order a fast,
proclaim a solemn assembly,
call the people together,
summon the community,
assemble the elders,
gather the children,
even the infants at the breast.
Let the bridegroom leave his bedroom
and the bride her alcove.
Between vestibule and altar let the priests,
the ministers of the Lord, lament.
Let them say,
"Spare your people, Lord!
Do not make your heritage a thing of shame,
a byword for the nations.
Why should it be said among the nations,
'Where is their God?' "

Then the Lord, jealous on behalf of his land,
took pity on his people.

The Lord spoke in answer to his people,
"Now I send you
corn and wine and oil,
until you have enough.
Never again shall I make you
a thing of shame for the nations."
This is the Word of the Lord.

130. Micah 6:1-4, 6-8   Do right and love mercy, and walk
humbly with your God.

A reading from the book of the prophet Micah
Now listen to what the Lord is saying:
Stand up and let the case begin
in the hearing of the mountains
and let the hills hear what you say.
Listen, you mountains, to the Lord's accusation,
give ear, you foundations of the earth,
for the Lord is accusing his people,
pleading against Israel:
My people, what have I done to you,

how have I been a burden to you? Answer me.
I brought you out of the land of Egypt,
I rescued you from the house of slavery;
I sent Moses to lead you,
with Aaron and Miriam.

"With what gift shall I come to the Lord's presence
and bow down before God on high?
Shall I come with holocausts,
with calves one year old?
Will he be pleased with rams by the thousand,
with libations of oil in torrents?
Must I give my first-born for what I have done wrong,
the fruit of my body for my own sin?"
—What is good has been explained to you, man;
this is what the Lord asks of you:
only this, to act justly,
to love tenderly
and to walk humbly with your God.
This is the Word of the Lord.

131. Micah 7:2-7, 18-20   The Lord will turn back and have
mercy on us; he will cast all our sins into the depths of the sea.

A reading from the book of the prophet Micah
The devout have vanished from the land:
there is not one honest man left.
All are lurking for blood,
every man hunting down his brother.
Their hands are skilled in evil:
the official demands . . . ,
the judge gives judgment for a bribe,
the man in power pronounces as he pleases.
Put no trust in a neighbor,
have no confidence in a friend;
to the woman who shares your bed
do not open your mouth.
For son insults father,
daughter defies mother,
daughter-in-law defies mother-in-law;
a man's enemies are those of his own household.
. . . among them, the best is like a briar,
the most honest a hedge of thorn.

Today will come their ordeal from the North,
now is the time for their confusion.

For my part, I look to the Lord,
my hope is in the God who will save me;
my God will hear me.

What god can compare with you: taking fault away,
pardoning crime,
not cherishing anger for ever
but delighting in showing mercy?
Once more have pity on us,
tread down our faults,
to the bottom of the sea
throw all our sins.
Grant Jacob your faithfulness,
and Abraham your mercy,
as you swore to our fathers
from the days of long ago.
This is the Word of the Lord.

132. Zechariah 1:1-6   Return to me, and I shall return to you.

A reading from the book of the prophet Zechariah
In the second year of Darius, in the eighth month,
    the word of the Lord was addressed
    to the prophet Zechariah (son of Berechiah),
    son of Iddo, as follows,
    "Cry out to the remnant of this people and say to them,
    the Lord Sabaoth says this:
    Return to me, and I will return to you,
    says the Lord Sabaoth.
Do not be like your ancestors,
    to whom the prophets in the past cried:
    the Lord Sabaoth says this:
    Turn back from your evil ways and evil deeds.
But—it is the Lord who speaks—
    they would not listen or pay attention to me.
Where are your ancestors now?
Are those prophets still alive?
Did not my words and my orders,
    with which I charged my servants the prophets,
    overtake your ancestors?
The Lord was stirred to anger against your ancestors."
This reduced them to such confusion that they said,

"The Lord Sabaoth has treated us as he resolved to do,
and as our ways and deeds deserved."
This is the Word of the Lord.

RESPONSORIAL PSALM

133. Psalm 13

R̷. (6a): **All my hope, O Lord, is in your loving kindness.**

How long, O Lord, will you forget me?
How long will you hide your face?
How long must I bear grief in my soul,
this sorrow in my heart day and night?
How long shall my enemy prevail?   R̷.

Look at me, answer me, Lord my God!
Give light to my eyes lest I fall asleep in death,
lest my enemy say: "I have overcome him";
lest my foes rejoice to see my fall.   R̷.

As for me, I trust in your merciful love.
Let my heart rejoice in your saving help:
Let me sing to the Lord for his goodness to me,
singing psalms to the name of the Lord, the Most High.   R̷.

134. Psalm 25

R̷. (16a): **Turn to me, Lord, and have mercy.**

To you, O Lord, I lift up my soul.
I trust you, let me not be disappointed;
do not let my enemies triumph.
Those who hope in you shall not be disappointed,
but only those who wantonly break faith.   R̷.

Lord, make me know your ways.
Lord, teach me your paths.
Make me walk in your truth, and teach me:
for you are God my savior.   R̷.

In you I hope all day long
because of your goodness, O Lord.
Remember your mercy, Lord,
and the love you have shown from of old.

Do not remember the sins of my youth.
In your love remember me.
R̯. (16a): Turn to me, Lord, and have mercy.

The Lord is good and upright.
He shows the path to those who stray,
He guides the humble in the right path;
He teaches his way to the poor.   R̯.

His ways are faithfulness and love
for those who keep his covenant and will.
Lord, for the sake of your name
forgive my guilt; for it is great.   R̯.

If anyone fears the Lord
he will show him the path he should choose.
His soul shall live in happiness
and his children shall possess the land.
The Lord's friendship is for those who revere him;
to them he reveals his covenant.   R̯.

My eyes are always on the Lord;
for he rescues my feet from the snare.
Turn to me and have mercy
for I am lonely and poor.   R̯.

Relieve the anguish of my heart
and set me free from my distress.
See my affliction and my toil
and take all my sins away.   R̯.

See how many are my foes;
how violent their hatred for me.
Preserve my life and rescue me.
Do not disappoint me, you are my refuge.
May innocence and uprightness protect me:
for my hope is in you, O Lord.
Redeem Israel, O God, from all its distress.   R̯.

135. Psalm 31:2-6

R̯. (6b): You have redeemed us, Lord, God of truth.

In you, O Lord, I take refuge.
Let me never be put to shame.

In your justice, set me free,
hear me and speedily rescue me.   R℞.

Be a rock of refuge for me,
a mighty stronghold to save me,
for you are my rock, my stronghold.
For your name's sake, lead me and guide me.   R℞.

Release me from the snares they have hidden,
for you are my refuge, Lord.
Into your hands I commend my spirit.
It is you who will redeem me, Lord.   R℞.

136. Psalm 32

R℞. (5c): **Lord, forgive the wrong I have done.**

Happy the man whose offence is forgiven,
whose sin is remitted.
O happy the man to whom the Lord
imputes no guilt,
in whose spirit is no guile.   R℞.

I kept it secret and my frame was wasted.
I groaned all day long
for night and day your hand
was heavy upon me.
Indeed, my strength was dried up
as by the summer's heat.   R℞.

But now I have acknowledged my sins;
my guilt I did not hide.
I said: "I will confess
my offence to the Lord."
And you, Lord, have forgiven
the guilt of my sin.   R℞.

So let every good man pray to you
in the time of need.
The floods of water may reach high
but him they shall not reach.
You are my hiding place, O Lord;
you save me from distress.
You surround me with cries of deliverance.   R℞.

I will instruct you and teach you
the way you should go;
I will give you counsel
with my eye upon you.
R̹. (5c): Lord, forgive the wrong I have done.

Be not like horse and mule, unintelligent,
needing bridle and bit,
else they will not approach you.
Many sorrows has the wicked
but he who trusts in the Lord,
loving mercy surrounds him.   R̹.

Rejoice, rejoice in the Lord,
exult, you just!
O come, ring out your joy,
all you upright of heart.   R̹.

137. Psalm 36

R̹. (8): How precious is your unfailing love, Lord.

Sin speaks to the sinner
in the depths of his heart.
There is no fear of God
before his eyes.   R̹.

He so flatters himself in his mind
that he knows not his guilt.
In his mouth are mischief and deceit.
All wisdom is gone.   R̹.

He plots the defeat of goodness
as he lies on his bed.
He has set his foot on evil ways,
he clings to what is evil.   R̹.

Your love, Lord, reaches to heaven;
your truth to the skies.
Your justice is like God's mountain,
your judgments like the deep.   R̹.

To both man and beast you give protection.
O Lord, how precious is your love.
My God, the sons of men
find refuge in the shelter of your wings.   R̹.

They feast on the riches of your house;
they drink from the stream of your delight.
In you is the source of life
and in your light we see light. ℟.

Keep on loving those who know you,
doing justice for upright hearts.
Let the foot of the proud not crush me
nor the hand of the wicked cast me out. ℟.

See how the evil-doers fall!
Flung down, they shall never arise. ℟.

138. Psalm 50: 7-8, 14-23

℟. (23b): **To the upright I will show the saving power of God.**

"Listen, my people, I will speak;
Israel, I will testify against you,
for I am God your God.
I accuse you, lay the charge before you.
I find no fault with your sacrifices,
your offerings are always before me. ℟.

Pay your sacrifice of thanksgiving to God
and render him your votive offerings.
Call on me in the day of distress.
I will free you and you shall honor me." ℟.

(But God says to the wicked:)
"But how can you recite my commandments
and take my covenant on your lips,
you who despise my law
and throw my words to the winds, ℟.

you who see a thief and go with him;
who throw in your lot with adulterers,
who unbridle your mouth for evil
and whose tongue is plotting crime, ℟.

you who sit and malign your brother
and slander your own mother's son.
You do this, and should I keep silence?
Do you think that I am like you? ℟.

Mark this, you who never think of God,
lest I seize you and you cannot escape;
a sacrifice of thanksgiving honors me
and I will show God's salvation to the upright."
℟. (23b): To the upright I will show the saving power of God.

139. Psalm 51

℟. (14a): Give back to me the joy of your salvation.

Have mercy on me, God, in your kindness.
In your compassion blot out my offence.
O wash me more and more from my guilt
and cleanse me from my sin.   ℟.

My offences truly I know them;
my sin is always before me.
Against you, you alone, have I sinned;
what is evil in your sight I have done.   ℟.

That you may be justified when you give sentence
and be without reproach when you judge.
O see, in guilt I was born,
a sinner was I conceived.   ℟.

Indeed you love truth in the heart;
then in the secret of my heart teach me wisdom
O purify me, then I shall be clean;
O wash me, I shall be whiter than snow.   ℟.

Make me hear rejoicing and gladness,
that the bones you have crushed may revive.
From my sins turn away your face
and blot out all my guilt.   ℟.

A pure heart create for me, O God,
put a steadfast spirit within me.
Do not cast me away from your presence,
nor deprive me of your holy spirit.   ℟.

Give me again the joy of your help;
with a spirit of fervor sustain me,
that I may teach transgressors your ways
and sinners may return to you.   ℟.

O rescue me, God, my helper,
and my tongue shall ring out your goodness.
O Lord, open my lips
and my mouth shall declare your praise.   ℟.

For in sacrifice you take no delight,
burnt offering from me you would refuse,
my sacrifice, a contrite spirit.
A humbled, contrite heart you will not spurn.   ℟.

In your goodness, show favor to Sion:
rebuild the walls of Jerusalem.
Then you will be pleased with lawful sacrifice,
holocausts offered on your altar.   ℟.

140. Psalm 73

℟. (28a): It is good for me to be with the Lord.

How good God is to Israel,
to those who are pure of heart.
Yet my feet came close to stumbling,
my steps had almost slipped
for I was filled with envy of the proud
when I saw how the wicked prosper.   ℟.

For them there are no pains;
their bodies are sound and sleek.
They have no share in men's sorrows;
they are not stricken like others.   ℟.

So they wear their pride like a necklace,
they clothe themselves with violence.
Their hearts overflow with malice,
their minds seethe with plots.   ℟.

They scoff; they speak with malice;
from on high they plan oppression.
They have set their mouths in the heavens
and their tongues dictate to the earth.   ℟.

So the people turn to follow them
and drink in all their words.
They say: "How can God know?

Does the Most High take any notice?"
Look at them, such are the wicked,
but untroubled, they grow in wealth.
R̸. (28a): It is good for me to be with the Lord.

How useless to keep my heart pure
and wash my hands in innocence,
when I was stricken all day long,
suffered punishment day after day. R̸.

Then I said: "If I should speak like that,
I should abandon the faith of your people."
I strove to fathom this problem,
too hard for my mind to understand,
until I pierced the mysteries of God
and understood what becomes of the wicked. R̸.

How slippery the paths on which you set them;
You make them slide to destruction.
How suddenly they come to their ruin,
wiped out, destroyed by terrors.
Like a dream one wakes from, O Lord,
when you wake you dismiss them as phantoms. R̸.

And so when my heart grew embittered
and when I was cut to the quick,
I was stupid and did not understand,
no better than a beast in your sight. R̸.

Yet I was always in your presence;
you were holding me by my right hand.
You will guide me by your counsel
and so you will lead me to glory. R̸.

What else have I in heaven but you?
Apart from you I want nothing on earth.
My body and my heart faint for joy;
God is my possession for ever. R̸.

All those who abandon you shall perish;
you will destroy all those who are faithless.
To be near God is my happiness.
I have made the Lord God my refuge.
I will tell of all your works
at the gates of the city of Sion. R̸.

141. Psalm 90

R℣. (14): **Fill us with your love, O Lord, and we will sing for joy!**

O Lord, you have been our refuge
from one generation to the next.
Before the mountains were born
or the earth or the world brought forth,
you are God, without beginning or end.   R℣.

You turn men back into dust
and say: "Go back, sons of men."
To your eyes a thousand years
are like yesterday, come and gone,
no more than a watch in the night.   R℣.

You sweep men away like a dream,
like grass which springs up in the morning.
In the morning it springs up and flowers:
by evening it withers and fades.   R℣.

So we are destroyed in your anger
struck with terror in your fury.
Our guilt lies open before you;
our secrets in the light of your face.   R℣.

All our days pass away in your anger.
Our life is over like a sigh.
Our span is seventy years
or eighty for those who are strong.   R℣.

And most of these are emptiness and pain.
They pass swiftly and we are gone.
Who understands the power of your anger
and fears the strength of your fury?   R℣.

Make us know the shortness of our life
that we may gain wisdom of heart.
Lord, relent! Is your anger for ever?
Show pity to your servants.   R℣.

In the morning, fill us with your love;
we shall exult and rejoice all our days.

Give us joy to balance our affliction
for the years when we knew misfortune.
℟. (14): Fill us with your love, O Lord, and we will sing for
joy!

Show forth your work to your servants;
let your glory shine on their children.
Let the favor of the Lord be upon us:
give success to the work of our hands,
give success to the work of our hands.   ℟.

142. Psalm 95

℟. (8a): If today you hear his voice, harden not your hearts.

Come, ring out our joy to the Lord;
hail the God who saves us.
Let us come before him, giving thanks,
with songs let us hail the Lord.   ℟.

A mighty God is the Lord,
a great king above all gods.
In his hand are the depths of the earth;
the heights of the mountains are his.
To him belongs the sea, for he made it,
and the dry land shaped by his hands.   ℟.

Come in; let us bow and bend low;
let us kneel before the God who made us
for he is our God and we
the people who belong to his pasture,
the flock that is led by his hand.   ℟.

O that to-day you would listen to his voice!
"Harden not your hearts as at Meribah,
as on that day at Massah in the desert
when your fathers put me to the test;
when they tried me, though they saw my work.   ℟.

For forty years I was wearied of these people
and I said: 'Their hearts are astray,
these people do not know my ways.'
Then I took an oath in my anger:
Never shall they enter my rest."   ℟.

143. Psalm 119:1, 10-13, 15-16

R̷. (1): **Happy are they who follow the law of the Lord!**

They are happy whose life is blameless,
who follow God's law!
I have sought you with all my heart:
let me not stray from your commands. R̷.

I treasure your promise in my heart
lest I sin against you.
Blessed are you, O Lord;
teach me your commands.
With my tongue I have recounted
the decrees of your lips. R̷.

I will ponder all your precepts
and consider your paths.
I take delight in your commands;
I will not forget your word. R̷.

144. Psalm 123

R̷. (2c): **Our eyes are fixed on the Lord.**

To you have I lifted up my eyes,
you who dwell in the heavens:
my eyes, like the eyes of slaves
on the hand of their lords.
Like the eyes of a servant
on the hand of her mistress,
so our eyes are on the Lord our God
till he show us his mercy. R̷.

Have mercy on us, Lord, have mercy.
We are filled with contempt.
Indeed all too full is our soul
with the scorn of the rich,
with the proud man's disdain. R̷.

145. Psalm 130

R̷. (7bc): **With the Lord there is mercy, and fullness of**
redemption.

Out of the depths I cry to you, O Lord,
Lord, hear my voice!
O let your ears be attentive
to the voice of my pleading.
℟. (2c): Our eyes are fixed on the Lord.

If you, O Lord, should mark our guilt,
Lord, who would survive?
But with you is found forgiveness:
for this we revere you.   ℟.

My soul is waiting for the Lord,
I count on his word.
My soul is longing for the Lord
more than watchman for daybreak.
Let the watchman count on daybreak
and Israel on the Lord.   ℟.

Because with the Lord there is mercy
and fullness of redemption,
Israel indeed he will redeem
from all its iniquity.   ℟.

146. Psalm 139:1-18, 23-24

℟. (23a): You have searched me, and you know me, Lord.

O Lord, you search me and you know me,
you know my resting and my rising,
you discern my purpose from afar.
You mark when I walk or lie down,
all my ways lie open to you.   ℟.

Before ever a word is on my tongue
you know it, O Lord, through and through.
Behind and before you besiege me,
your hand ever laid upon me.
Too wonderful for me, this knowledge,
too high, beyond my reach.   ℟.

O where can I go from your spirit,
or where can I flee from your face?
If I climb the heavens, you are there.
If I lie in the grave, you are there.   ℟.

If I take the wings of the dawn
and dwell at the sea's furthest end,
even there your hand would lead me,
your right hand would hold me fast.   R⁷.

If I say: "Let the darkness hide me
and the light around me be night,"
even darkness is not dark for you
and the night is as clear as the day.   R⁷.

For it was you who created my being,
knit me together in my mother's womb.
I thank you for the wonder of my being,
for the wonders of all your creation.   R⁷.

Already you knew my soul,
my body held no secret from you
when I was being fashioned in secret
and moulded in the depths of the earth.   R⁷.

Your eyes saw all my actions,
they were all of them written in your book;
every one of my days was decreed
before one of them came into being.   R⁷.

To me, how mysterious your thoughts,
the sum of them not to be numbered!
If I count them, they are more than the sand;
to finish, I must be eternal, like you.   R⁷.

O search me, God, and know my heart.
O test me and know my thoughts.
See that I follow not the wrong path
and lead me in the path of life eternal.   R⁷.

147. Psalm 143: 1-11

R⁷. (10): Teach me to do your will, my God.

Lord, listen to my prayer:
turn your ear to my appeal.
You are faithful, you are just; give answer.
Do not call your servant to judgment
for no one is just in your sight.   R⁷.

The enemy pursues my soul;
he has crushed my life to the ground;
he has made me dwell in darkness
like the dead, long forgotten.
Therefore my spirit fails;
my heart is numb within me.
℞. (10): Teach me to do your will, my God.

I remember the days that are past:
I ponder all your works.
I muse on what your hand has wrought
and to you I stretch out my hands.
Like a parched land my soul thirsts for you.   ℞.

Lord, make haste and answer;
for my spirit fails within me.
Do not hide your face
lest I become like those in the grave.   ℞.

In the morning let me know your love
for I put my trust in you.
Make me know the way I should walk:
to you I lift up my soul.   ℞.

Rescue me, Lord, from my enemies;
I have fled to you for refuge.
Teach me to do your will
for you, O Lord, are my God.
Let your good spirit guide me
in ways that are level and smooth.   ℞.

For your name's sake, Lord, save my life;
in your justice save my soul from distress.   ℞.

READINGS FROM THE NEW TESTAMENT

148. Romans 3:22-26   All men are justified by the
gift of God through redemption in Christ Jesus.

A reading from the letter of Paul to the Romans
It is the same justice of God
   that now comes through faith to everyone,
   Jew and pagan alike, who believes in Jesus Christ.
Both Jew and pagan sinned and forfeited God's glory,

and both are justified through the free gift of his grace
by being redeemed in Christ Jesus
who was appointed by God
to sacrifice his life
so as to win reconciliation through faith.
In this way God makes his justice known; first, for the past,
    when sins went unpunished because he held his hand,
    then, for the present age,
    by showing positively that he is just,
    and that he justifies everyone who believes in Jesus.
This is the Word of the Lord.

149. Romans 5:6-11   We give glory in God through our Lord
Jesus Christ, through whom we have received reconciliation.

A reading from the letter of Paul to the Romans
We were still helpless when at his appointed moment
    Christ died for sinful men.
It is not easy to die even for a good man—
    though of course for someone really worthy,
    a man might be prepared to die—
    but what proves that God loves us
    is that Christ died for us while we were still sinners.
Having died to make us righteous,
    is it likely that he would now fail
    to save us from God's anger?
When we were reconciled to God by the death of his Son,
    we were still enemies; now that we have been reconciled,
    surely we may count on being saved by the life of his Son?
Not merely because we have been reconciled
    but because we are filled with joyful trust in God,
    through our Lord Jesus Christ,
    through whom we have already gained our reconciliation.
This is the Word of the Lord.

150. Romans 6:2b-13   Consider yourselves dead to sin but
alive to God.

A reading from the letter of Paul to the Romans
We are dead to sin, so how can we continue to live in it?
You have been taught that when we were baptized in Christ Jesus
    we were baptized in his death;
    in other words, when we were baptized

we went into the tomb with him and joined him in death,
so that as Christ was raised from the dead by the Father's glory,
we too might live a new life.

If in union with Christ we have imitated his death,
we shall also imitate him in his resurrection.
We must realize that our former selves
have been crucified with him
to destroy this sinful body
and to free us from the slavery of sin.
When a man dies, of course, he has finished with sin.

But we believe that having died with Christ
we shall return to life with him:
Christ, as we know,
having been raised from the dead will never die again.
Death has no power over him any more.
When he died, he died, once for all, to sin,
so his life now is life with God;
and in that way, you too must consider yourselves
to be dead to sin but alive for God in Christ Jesus.

That is why you must not let sin reign in your mortal bodies
or command your obedience to bodily passions,
why you must not let any part of your body
turn into an unholy weapon fighting on the side of sin;
you should, instead, offer yourselves to God
and consider yourselves dead men, brought back to life;
you should make every part of your body into a weapon
fighting on the side of God.
This is the Word of the Lord.

151. Romans 6:16-23   The wages of sin is death; the gift of
God is eternal life in Christ Jesus our Lord.

A reading from the letter of Paul to the Romans
You know that if you agree to serve and obey a master
you become his slaves.
You cannot be slaves of sin that leads to death
and at the same time slaves of obedience
that leads to righteousness.
You were once slaves of sin,
but thank God you submitted without reservation

to the creed you were taught.
You may have been freed from the slavery of sin,
  but only to become "slaves" of righteousness.
If I may use human terms to help your natural weakness:
  as once you put your bodies
  at the service of vice and immorality,
  so now you must put them at the service of righteousness
  for your sanctification.

When you were slaves of sin,
  you felt no obligation to righteousness,
  and what did you get from this?
Nothing but experiences that now make you blush,
  since that sort of behavior ends in death.
Now, however, you have been set free from sin,
  you have been made slaves of God,
  and you get a reward leading to your sanctification
  and ending in eternal life.
For the wage paid by sin is death;
  the present given by God
  is eternal life in Christ Jesus our Lord.
This is the Word of the Lord.

152. Romans 7:14-25   Unhappy man that I am! Who will free
me? Thanks to God through Jesus Christ our Lord.

The Law, of course, as we all know, is spiritual;
  but I am unspiritual; I have been sold as a slave to sin.
I cannot understand my own behavior.
I fail to carry out the things I want to do,
  and I find myself doing the very things I hate.
When I act against my own will,
  that means I have a self that acknowledges
  that the Law is good,
  and so the thing behaving in that way is not my self
  but sin living in me.
The fact is, I know of nothing good living in me—
  living, that is, in my unspiritual self—
  for though the will to do good is in me,
  the performance is not,
  with the result that instead of doing the good things I want to do,
  I carry out the sinful things I do not want.

When I act against my will, then,
  it is not my true self doing it, but sin which lives in me.

In fact, this seems to be the rule,
  that every single time I want to do good
  it is something evil that comes to hand.
In my inmost self I dearly love God's Law,
  but I can see that my body follows a different law
  that battles against the law which my reason dictates.
This is what makes me a prisoner of that law of sin
  which lives inside my body.

What a wretched man I am!
Who will rescue me from this body doomed to death?
Thanks be to God through Jesus Christ our Lord!

In short, it is I who with my reason serve the Law of God,
  and no less I who serve in my unspiritual self the law of sin.
This is the Word of the Lord.

153. Romans 12:1-2, 9-19   Be transformed by the renewal of your mind.

A reading from the letter of Paul to the Romans
Think of God's mercy, my brothers, and worship him,
  I beg you, in a way that is worthy of thinking beings,
  by offering your living bodies as a holy sacrifice,
  truly pleasing to God.
Do not model yourselves
  on the behavior of the world around you,
  but let your behavior change, modelled by your new mind.
This is the only way to discover the will of God
  and know what is good, what it is that God wants,
  what is the perfect thing to do.

Do not let your love be a pretence,
  but sincerely prefer good to evil.
Love each other as much as brothers should,
  and have a profound respect for each other.
Work for the Lord with untiring effort
  and with great earnestness of spirit.
If you have hope, this will make you cheerful.
Do not give up if trials come; and keep on praying.
If any of the saints are in need you must share with them;
  and you should make hospitality your special care.

Bless those who persecute you: never curse them, bless them.
Rejoice with those who rejoice
  and be sad with those in sorrow.
Treat everyone with equal kindness;
  never be condescending
  but make real friends with the poor.
Do not allow yourself to become self-satisfied.
Never repay evil with evil but let everyone see
  that you are interested only in the highest ideals.
Do all you can to live at peace with everyone.
Never try to get revenge;
  leave that, my friends, to God's anger.
As scripture says:
  Vengeance is mine—
  I will pay them back, the Lord promises.
This is the Word of the Lord.

154. Romans 13:8-14 Let us cast away the works of darkness and put on the weapons of light.

A reading from the letter of Paul to the Romans
Avoid getting into debt, except the debt of mutual love.
If you love your fellow men
  you have carried out your obligations.
All the commandments:
  You shall not commit adultery, you shall not kill,
  you shall not steal, you shall not covet,
  and so on, are summed up in this single command:
  You must love your neighbor as yourself.
Love is the one thing that cannot hurt your neighbor;
  that is why it is the answer
  to every one of the commandments.

Besides, you know "the time" has come:
  you must wake up now:
  our salvation is even nearer
  than it was when we were converted.
The night is almost over, it will be daylight soon.
  —Let us give up all the things we prefer to do
  under cover of the dark;
  let us arm ourselves and appear in the light.
Let us live decently as people do in the daytime:
  no drunken orgies, no promiscuity or licentiousness,

and no wrangling or jealousy.
Let your armor be the Lord Jesus Christ;
   forget about satisfying your bodies with all their cravings.
This is the Word of the Lord.

155. 2 Corinthians 5:17-21   God reconciled the world to himself through Christ.

A reading from the second letter of Paul to the Corinthians
For anyone who is in Christ, there is a new creation;
   the old creation has gone, and now the new one is here.
It is all God's work.
It was God who reconciled us to himself through Christ
   and gave us the work of handing on this reconciliation.
In other words,
   God in Christ was reconciling the world to himself,
   not holding men's faults against them,
   and he has entrusted to us the news that they are reconciled.
So we are ambassadors for Christ;
   it is as though God were appealing through us,
   and the appeal that we make in Christ's name is:
   be reconciled to God.
For our sake God made the sinless one into sin,
   so that in him we might become the goodness of God.
This is the Word of the Lord.

156. Galatians 5:16-24   You cannot belong to Christ unless you crucify the flesh with its passions and concupiscence.

A reading from the letter of Paul to the Galatians
Let me put it like this:
   if you are guided by the Spirit
   you will be in no danger of yielding to self-indulgence,
   since self-indulgence is the opposite of the Spirit,
   the Spirit is totally against such a thing,
   and it is precisely because the two are so opposed
   that you do not always carry out your good intentions.
If you are led by the Spirit, no law can touch you.
When self-indulgence is at work the results are obvious:
   fornication, gross indecency and sexual irresponsibility;
   idolatry and sorcery;
   feuds and wrangling, jealousy, bad temper and quarrels;

disagreements, factions, envy;
 drunkenness, orgies and similar things.
I warn you now, as I warned you before:
 those who behave like this
 will not inherit the kingdom of God.
What the Spirit brings is very different:
 love, joy, peace, patience,
 kindness, goodness, trustfulness, gentleness and self-control.
There can be no law against things like that, of course.
You cannot belong to Christ Jesus
 unless you crucify all self-indulgent passions and desires.
This is the Word of the Lord.

157. Ephesians 2:1-10 When we were dead to sin, God, on
account of his great love for us, brought us to life in Christ.

A reading from the letter of Paul to the Ephesians
And you were dead, through the crimes and the sins
 in which you used to live
 when you were following the way of this world,
 obeying the ruler who governs the air,
 the spirit who is at work in the rebellious.
We all were among them too in the past, living sensual lives,
 ruled entirely by our own physical desires and our own ideas;
 so that by nature we were as much under God's anger
 as the rest of the world.
But God loved us with so much love
 that he was generous with his mercy:
 when we were dead through our sins,
 he brought us to life with Christ—
 it is through grace that you have been saved—
 and raised us up with him
 and gave us a place with him in heaven, in Christ Jesus.

This was to show for all ages to come,
 through his goodness toward us in Christ Jesus,
 how infinitely rich he is in grace.
Because it is by grace that you have been saved,
 through faith; not by anything of your own,
 but by a gift from God;
 not by anything that you have done,
 so that nobody can claim the credit.

We are God's work of art,
  created in Christ Jesus to live the good life
  as from the beginning he had meant us to live it.
This is the Word of the Lord.

158. Ephesians 4:1-3, 17-32   Renew yourself and put on the new man.

A reading from the letter of Paul to the Ephesians
I, the prisoner in the Lord, implore you therefore
  to lead a life worthy of your vocation.
Bear with one another charitably,
  in complete selflessness, gentleness and patience.
Do all you can to preserve the unity of the Spirit
  by the peace that binds you together.

In particular, I want to urge you in the name of the Lord,
  not to go on living the aimless kind of life that pagans live.
Intellectually they are in the dark,
  and they are estranged from the life of God,
  without knowledge because they have shut their hearts to it.
Their sense of right and wrong once dulled,
  they have abandoned themselves to sexuality
  and eagerly pursue a career of indecency of every kind.
Now that is hardly the way you have learned from Christ,
  unless you failed to hear him properly
  when you were taught what the truth is in Jesus.
You must give up your old way of life;
  you must put aside your old self,
  which gets corrupted by following illusory desires.
Your mind must be renewed by a spiritual revolution
  so that you can put on the new self
  that has been created in God's way,
  in the goodness and holiness of the truth.

So from now on, there must be no more lies:
  You must speak the truth to one another,
  since we are all parts of one another.
Even if you are angry, you must not sin:
  never let the sun set on your anger
  or else you will give the devil a foothold.
Anyone who was a thief must stop stealing:

he should try to find some useful manual work instead,
   and be able to do some good by helping others
   that are in need.
Guard against foul talk:
   let your words be for the improvement of others,
   as occasion offers, and do good to your listeners,
   otherwise you will only be grieving the Holy Spirit of God
   who has marked you with his seal
   for you to be set free when the day comes.
Never have grudges against others, or lose your temper,
   or raise your voice to anybody, or call each other names,
   or allow any sort of spitefulness.
Be friends with one another, and kind,
   forgiving each other as readily as God forgave you in Christ.
This is the Word of the Lord.

159. Ephesians 5:1-14   You were once in darkness; now you
are light in the Lord, so walk as children of light.

A reading from the letter of Paul to the Ephesians
Try, then, to imitate God, as children of his that he loves,
   and follow Christ by loving as he loved you,
   giving himself up in our place
   as a fragrant offering and a sacrifice to God.
Among you there must be not even a mention
   of fornication or impurity in any of its forms,
   or promiscuity: this would hardly become the saints!
There must be no coarseness, or salacious talk and jokes—
   all this is wrong for you;
   raise your voices in thanksgiving instead.
For you can be quite certain that nobody who actually indulges
   in fornication or impurity or promiscuity—
   which is worshiping a false god—
   can inherit anything of the kingdom of God.
Do not let anyone deceive you with empty arguments:
   it is for this loose living that God's anger comes down
   on those who rebel against him.
Make sure that you are not included with them.
You were darkness once, but now you are light in the Lord;
   be like children of light, for the effects of the light
   are seen in complete goodness and right living and truth.
Try to discover what the Lord wants of you,

having nothing to do with the futile works of darkness
but exposing them by contrast.
The things which are done in secret
are things that people are ashamed even to speak of;
but anything exposed by the light will be illuminated
and anything illuminated turns into light.
That is why it is said:

Wake up from your sleep,
rise from the dead,
and Christ will shine on you.
This is the Word of the Lord.

160. Ephesians 6:10-18   Put God's armor on so that you will
be able to stand firm against evil.

A reading from the letter of Paul to the Ephesians
Finally, grow strong in the Lord, with the strength of his power.
Put God's armor on so as to be able to resist the devil's tactics.
For it is not against human enemies that we have to struggle,
but against the Sovereignties and the Powers
who originate the darkness in this world,
the spiritual army of evil in the heavens.
That is why you must rely on God's armor,
or you will not be able to put up any resistance
when the worst happens,
or have enough resources to hold your ground.

So stand your ground, with truth buckled round your waist,
and integrity for a breastplate,
wearing for shoes on your feet
the eagerness to spread the gospel of peace
and always carrying the shield of faith so that you can use it
to put out the burning arrows of the evil one.
And then you must accept salvation from God to be your helmet
and receive the word of God from the Spirit to use as a sword.

Pray all the time, asking for what you need,
praying in the Spirit on every possible occasion.
Never get tired of staying awake to pray for all the saints.
This is the Word of the Lord.

161. Colossians 3:1-10, 12-17   If you were raised to life with Christ, aspire to the realm above. Put to death what remains in this earthly life.

A reading from the letter of Paul to the Colossians
Since you have been brought back to true life with Christ,
   you must look for the things that are in heaven,
   where Christ is, sitting at God's right hand.
Let your thoughts be on heavenly things,
   not on the things that are on the earth,
   because you have died,
and now the life you have is hidden with Christ in God.
But when Christ is revealed—and he is your life—
   you too will be revealed in all your glory with him.

That is why you must kill everything in you
   that belongs only to earthly life:
   fornication, impurity, guilty passion, evil desires
   and especially greed,
   which is the same thing as worshiping a false god;
   all this is the sort of behavior that makes God angry.
And it is the way in which you used to live
   when you were surrounded by people doing the same thing,
   but now you, of all people, must give all these things up:
   getting angry, being bad-tempered, spitefulness,
   abusive language and dirty talk;
   and never tell each other lies.
You have stripped off your old behavior with your old self,
   and you have put on a new self
   which will progress toward true knowledge
   the more it is renewed in the image of its creator;

You are God's chosen race, his saints;
   he loves you,
   and you should be clothed in sincere compassion,
   in kindness and humility, gentleness and patience.
Bear with one another;
   forgive each other as soon as a quarrel begins.
The Lord has forgiven you; now you must do the same.
Over all these clothes,
   to keep them together and complete them, put on love.
And may the peace of Christ reign in your hearts,

because it is for this that you were called together
as parts of one body.
Always be thankful.

Let the message of Christ, in all its richness,
find a home with you.
Teach each other, and advise each other, in all wisdom.
With gratitude in your hearts
sing psalms and hymns and inspired songs to God;
and never say or do anything
except in the name of the Lord Jesus,
giving thanks to God the Father through him.
This is the Word of the Lord.

162. Hebrews 12:1-5   You have not resisted to the point of
shedding your blood in your struggle against sin.

A reading from the letter to the Hebrews
With so many witnesses in a great cloud on every side of us,
we too, then, should throw off everything that hinders us,
especially the sin that clings so easily,
and keep running steadily in the race we have started.
Let us not lose sight of Jesus,
who leads us in our faith and brings it to perfection:
for the sake of the joy which was still in the future,
he endured the cross, disregarding the shamefulness of it,
and from now on has taken his place
at the right of God's throne.
Think of the way he stood such opposition from sinners
and then you will not give up for want of courage.
In the fight against sin,
you have not yet had to keep fighting to the point of death.

Have you forgotten that encouraging text
in which you are addressed as sons?
My son, when the Lord corrects you, do not treat it lightly;
but do not get discouraged when he reprimands you.
This is the Word of the Lord.

163. James 1:22-27   Be doers of the word and not merely
listeners.

A reading from the letter of James

But you must do what the word tells you,
  and not just listen to it and deceive yourselves.
To listen to the word and not obey
  is like looking at your own features in a mirror and then,
  after a quick look, going off
  and immediately forgetting what you looked like.
But the man who looks steadily at the perfect law of freedom
  and makes that his habit—not listening and then forgetting,
  but actively putting it into practice—
  will be happy in all that he does.

Nobody must imagine that he is religious
  while he still goes on deceiving himself
  and not keeping control over his tongue;
  anyone who does this has the wrong idea of religion.
Pure, unspoilt religion, in the eyes of God our Father is this;
  coming to the help of orphans
  and widows when they need it,
  and keeping oneself uncontaminated by the world.
This is the Word of the Lord.

164. James 2:14-26   What use is it if someone says that he
believes and does not manifest it in works?

A reading from the letter of James
Take the case, my brothers, of someone
  who has never done a single good act
  but claims that he has faith.
Will that faith save him?
If one of the brothers or one of the sisters
  is in need of clothes and has not enough food to live on,
  and one of you says to them, "I wish you well;
  keep yourself warm and eat plenty,"
  without giving them these bare necessities of life,
  then what good is that?
Faith is like that:
  if good works do not go with it, it is quite dead.

This is the way to talk to people of that kind:
  "You say you have faith and I have good deeds;
  I will prove to you that I have faith
  by showing you my good deeds—
  now you prove to me that you have faith
  without any good deeds to show.

You believe in one God—that is creditable enough,
  but the demons have the same belief,
  and they tremble with fear.
Do realize, you senseless man,
  that faith without good deeds is useless.
You surely know that Abraham our father
  was justified by his deed,
  because he offered his son Isaac on the altar?
There you see it: faith and deeds were working together;
  his faith became perfect by what he did.
This is what scripture really means when it says:
  Abraham put his faith in God,
  and this was counted as making him justified;
  and that is why he was called 'the friend of God.' "

You see now that it is by doing something good,
  and not only by believing, that a man is justified.
There is another example of the same kind:
Rahab the prostitute, justified by her deeds
  because she welcomed the messengers
  and showed them a different way to leave.
A body dies when it is separated from the spirit,
  and in the same way
  faith is dead if it is separated from good deeds.
  This is the Word of the Lord.

165. James 3:1-12   If someone does not offend in word, he is a
perfect man.

A reading from the letter of James
Only a few of you, my brothers, should be teachers,
  bearing in mind that those of us who teach
  can expect a stricter judgment.

After all, every one of us does something wrong,
  over and over again;
  the only man who could reach perfection
  would be someone who never said anything wrong—
  he would be able to control every part of himself.
Once we put a bit into the horse's mouth,
  to make it do what we want,
  we have the whole animal under our control.

Or think of ships: no matter how big they are,
  even if a gale is driving them,
  the man at the helm can steer them anywhere he likes
  by controlling a tiny rudder.
So is the tongue only a tiny part of the body,
  but it can proudly claim that it does great things.
Think how small a flame can set fire to a huge forest;
  the tongue is a flame like that.
Among all the parts of the body,
  the tongue is a whole wicked world in itself:
  it infects the whole body;
  catching fire itself from hell,
  it sets fire to the whole wheel of creation.
Wild animals and birds, reptiles and fish
  can all be tamed by man, and often are;
  but nobody can tame the tongue—
  it is a pest that will not keep still, full of deadly poison.
We use it to bless the Lord and Father,
  but we also use it to curse men who are made in God's image:
  the blessing and the curse come out of the same mouth.
My brothers, this must be wrong—
  does any water supply give a flow
  of fresh water and salt water out of the same pipe?
Can a fig tree give you olives, my brothers, or a vine give figs?
No more can sea water give you fresh water.
This is the Word of the Lord.

166. 1 Peter 1:13-23 You have been redeemed not by perishable goods, gold or silver, but by the precious blood of Jesus Christ.

A reading from the first letter of Peter
Free your minds, then, of encumbrances;
  control them, and put your trust in nothing but the grace
  that will be given you when Jesus Christ is revealed.
Do not behave in the way that you liked to
  before you learned the truth;
  make a habit of obedience:
  be holy in all you do,
  since it is the Holy One who has called you,
  and scripture says: Be holy, for I am holy.

If you are acknowledging as your Father
    one who has no favorites
    and judges everyone according to what he has done,
    you must be scrupulously careful
    as long as you are living away from your home.
Remember, the ransom that was paid to free you
    from the useless way of life your ancestors handed down
    was not paid in anything corruptible,
    neither in silver nor gold,
    but in the precious blood of a lamb without spot or stain,
    namely Christ;
    who, though known since before the world was made,
    has been revealed only in our time,
    the end of the ages, for your sake.
Through him you now have faith in God,
    who raised him from the dead
    and gave him glory for that very reason—
    so that you would have faith and hope in God.

You have been obedient to the truth and purified your souls
    until you can love like brothers,
    in sincerity;
    let your love for each other be real and from the heart—
    your new birth was not from any mortal seed
    but from the everlasting word of the living and eternal God.
This is the Word of the Lord.

167. 2 Peter 1:3-11   Be careful so that you may make firm your
calling and election.

A reading from the second letter of Peter
By his divine power, he has given us all the things
    that we need for life and for true devotion,
    bringing us to know God himself,
    who has called us by his own glory and goodness.
In making these gifts, he has given us the guarantee
    of something very great and wonderful to come:
    through them you will be able to share the divine nature
    and to escape corruption in a world that is sunk in vice.
But to attain this, you will have to do your utmost yourselves,
    adding goodness to the faith that you have,
    understanding to your goodness,
    self-control to your understanding,

patience to your self-control, true devotion to your patience,
kindness toward your fellow men to your devotion,
and, to this kindness, love.
If you have a generous supply of these,
they will not leave you ineffectual or unproductive:
they will bring you to a real knowledge
of our Lord Jesus Christ.
But without them a man is blind or else short-sighted;
he has forgotten how his past sins were washed away.
Brothers, you have been called and chosen:
work all the harder to justify it.
If you do all these things
there is no danger that you will ever fall away.
In this way you will be granted admittance
into the eternal kingdom of our Lord and savior Jesus Christ.
This is the Word of the Lord.

168. 1 John 1:5-10; 2:1-2   If we confess our sins, he is faithful
and just and will forgive our sins and cleanse us from all
injustice.

A reading from the first letter of John
This is what we have heard from him,
and the message that we are announcing to you:
God is light; there is no darkness in him at all.
If we say that we are in union with God
while we are living in darkness,
we are lying because we are not living the truth.
But if we live our lives in the light,
as he is in the light,
we are in union with one another,
and the blood of Jesus, his Son,
purifies us from all sin.

If we say we have no sin in us,
we are deceiving ourselves
and refusing to admit the truth;
but if we acknowledge our sins,
then God who is faithful and just
will forgive our sins and purify us
from everything that is wrong.
To say that we have never sinned
is to call God a liar
and to show that his word is not in us.

I am writing this, my children,
to stop you sinning;
but if anyone should sin,
we have our advocate with the Father,
Jesus Christ, who is just;
he is the sacrifice that takes our sins away,
and not only ours,
but the whole world's.
This is the Word of the Lord.

169. 2 John 2:3-11   Whoever hates his brother remains in
darkness.

A reading from the second letter of John
We can be sure that we know God
only by keeping his commandments.
Anyone who says, "I know him,"
and does not keep his commandments,
is a liar,
refusing to admit the truth.
But when anyone does obey what he has said,
God's love comes to perfection in him.
We can be sure
that we are in God
only when the one who claims to be living in him
is living the same kind of life as Christ lived.
My dear people,
this is not a new commandment that I am writing to tell you,
but an old commandment
that you were given from the beginning,
the original commandment
which was the message brought to you.
Yet in another way, what I am writing to you,
and what is being carried out in your lives as it was in his,
is a new commandment;
because the night is over
and the real light is already shining.
Anyone who claims to be in the light
but hates his brother
is still in the dark.
But anyone who loves his brother is living in the light
and need not be afraid of stumbling;
unlike the man who hates his brother and is in the darkness,
not knowing where he is going,

because it is too dark to see.
This is the Word of the Lord.

170. 1 John 3:1-24   We know that we have crossed over from
death to life because we love our brothers.

A reading from the first letter of John
Think of the love that the Father has lavished on us,
by letting us be called God's children;
and that is what we are.
Because the world refused to acknowledge him,
therefore it does not acknowledge us.
My dear people, we are already the children of God
but what we are to be in the future has not yet been revealed;
all we know is, that when it is revealed
we shall be like him
because we shall see him as he really is.

Surely everyone who entertains this hope
must purify himself, must try to be as pure as Christ.
Anyone who sins at all
breaks the law,
because to sin is to break the law.
Now you know that he appeared in order to abolish sin,
and that in him there is no sin;
anyone who lives in God does not sin,
and anyone who sins
has never seen him or known him.
My children, do not let anyone lead you astray:
to live a holy life
is to be holy just as he is holy;
to lead a sinful life is to belong to the devil,
since the devil was a sinner from the beginning.
It was to undo all that the devil has done
that the Son of God appeared.
No one who has been begotten by God sins;
because God's seed remains inside him,
he cannot sin when he has been begotten by God.

In this way we distinguish the children of God
from the children of the devil:
anybody not living a holy life
and not loving his brother
is no child of God's.

This is the message
as you heard it from the beginning:
that we are to love one another;
not to be like Cain, who belonged to the Evil One
and cut his brother's throat;
cut his brother's throat simply for this reason,
that his own life was evil and his brother lived a good life.
You must not be surprised, brothers,
when the world hates you;
we have passed out of death and into life,
and of this we can be sure
because we love our brothers.
If you refuse to love, you must remain dead;
to hate your brother is to be a murderer,
and murderers, as you know, do not have eternal life in them.
This has taught us love—
that he gave up his life for us;
and we, too, ought to give up our lives for our brothers.
If a man who was rich enough in this world's goods
saw that one of his brothers was in need,
but closed his heart to him,
how could the love of God be living in him?
My children,
our love is not to be just words or mere talk,
but something real and active;
only by this can we be certain
that we are children of the truth
and be able to quiet our conscience in his presence,
whatever accusations it may raise against us,
because God is greater than our conscience
and he knows everything.
My dear people,
if we cannot be condemned by our own conscience,
we need not be afraid in God's presence,
and whatever we ask him,
we shall receive,
because we keep his commandments
and live the kind of life that he wants.
His commandments are these:
that we believe in the name of his Son Jesus Christ
and that we love one another
as he told us to.
Whoever keeps his commandments
lives in God and God lives in him.

We know that he lives in us
by the Spirit that he has given us.
This is the Word of the Lord.

171. 1 John 4:16-21   God is love, and he who lives in love,
lives in God, and God in him.

A reading from the first letter of John
We ourselves have known and put our faith in
God's love toward ourselves.
God is love
and anyone who lives in love lives in God,
and God lives in him.
Love will come to its perfection in us
when we can face the day of Judgment without fear;
because even in this world
we have become as he is.
In love there can be no fear,
but fear is driven out by perfect love:
because to fear is to expect punishment,
and anyone who is afraid is still imperfect in love.
We are to love, then,
because he loved us first.
Anyone who says, "I love God,"
and hates his brother,
is a liar,
since a man who does not love the brother that he can see
cannot love God, whom he has never seen.
So this is the commandment that he has given us,
that anyone who loves God must also love his brother.
This is the Word of the Lord.

172. Revelation 2:1-5   Do penance and return to your former
ways.

A reading from the book of Revelation
Write to the angel of the church in Ephesus and say,
   "Here is the message
   of the one who holds the seven stars in his right hand
   and who lives surrounded by the seven golden lamp-stands:
   I know all about you:
   how hard you work and how much you put up with.
I know you cannot stand wicked men,

and how you tested the impostors
who called themselves apostles
and proved they were liars.
I know, too, that you have patience,
and have suffered for my name without growing tired.
Nevertheless, I have this complaint to make;
you have less love now than you used to.
Think where you were before you fell;
repent, and do as you used to at first,
or else, if you will not repent,
I shall come to you and take your lamp-stand from its place."
This is the Word of the Lord.

173. Revelation 3:14-22   Because you are lukewarm, neither
hot or cold, I will vomit you out of my mouth.

A reading from the book of Revelation
Write to the angel of the church in Laodicea and say,
"Here is the message of the Amen,
the faithful, the true witness,
the ultimate source of God's creation:
I know all about you: how you are neither cold nor hot.
I wish you were one or the other,
but since you are neither, but only lukewarm,
I will spit you out of my mouth.
You say to yourself, "I am rich,
I have made a fortune, and have everything I want,"
never realizing that you are wretchedly and pitiably poor,
and blind and naked too.
I warn you, buy from me the gold
that has been tested in the fire to make you really rich,
and white robes to clothe you
and cover your shameful nakedness,
and eye ointment to put on your eyes
so that you are able to see.
I am the one who reproves and disciplines all those he loves:
so repent in real earnest.
Look, I am standing at the door, knocking.
If one of you hears me calling and opens the door,
I will come in to share his meal, side by side with him.
Those who prove victorious I will allow to share my throne,
just as I was victorious myself
and took my place with my Father on his throne.

If anyone has ears to hear,
   let him listen to what the Spirit is saying to the churches."
This is the Word of the Lord.

174. Revelation 20:11-15   All have been judged according to
their works.

A reading from the book of Revelation
Then I saw a great white throne
   and the one who was sitting on it.
In his presence, earth and sky vanished, leaving no trace.
I saw the dead, both great and small,
   standing in front of his throne,
   while the book of life was opened,
   and other books opened
   which were the record of what they had done in their lives,
   by which the dead were judged.

The sea gave up all the dead who were in it;
   Death and Hades were emptied of the dead that were in them;
   and every one was judged
   according to the way in which he had lived.
Then Death and Hades were thrown into the burning lake.
This burning lake is the second death;
   and anybody
   whose name could not be found written in the book of life
   was thrown into the burning lake.
This is the Word of the Lord.

175. Revelation 21:1-8   Whoever conquers will inherit all this,
and I will be his God, and he will be my son.

A reading from the book of Revelation
Then I saw a new heaven and a new earth;
   the first heaven and the first earth had disappeared now,
   and there was no longer any sea.
I saw the holy city, and the new Jerusalem,
   coming down from God out of heaven,
   as beautiful as a bride all dressed for her husband.
Then I heard a loud voice call from the throne,
   "You see this city?
Here God lives among men.

He will make his home among them;
  they shall be his people, and he will be their God;
  his name is God-with-them.
He will wipe away all tears from their eyes;
  there will be no more death,
  and no more mourning or sadness.
The world of the past has gone."

Then the One sitting on the throne spoke:
  "Now I am making the whole of creation new," he said.
"Write this: that what I am saying is sure and will come true."
And then he said, "It is already done.
I am the Alpha and the Omega, the Beginning and the End.
I will give water from the well of life
  free to anybody who is thirsty;
  it is the rightful inheritance of the one who proves victorious;
  and I will be his God and he a son to me.
But the legacy for cowards,
  for those who break their word, or worship obscenities,
  for murderers and fornicators, and for fortune-tellers,
  idolaters or any other sort of liars,
  is the second death in the burning lake of sulphur."
This is the Word of the Lord.

GOSPEL

176. Matthew 3:1-12   Repent, for the kingdom of heaven is
close at hand.

✝ A reading from the holy gospel according to Matthew
In due course John the Baptist appeared;
  he preached in the wilderness of Judaea
  and this was his message:
  "Repent, for the kingdom of heaven is close at hand."
This was the man the prophet Isaiah spoke of when he said:

  A voice cries in the wilderness:
  Prepare a way for the Lord,
  make his paths straight.

This man John wore a garment made of camel-hair
  with a leather belt round his waist,
  and his food was locusts and wild honey.
Then Jerusalem and all Judaea and the whole Jordan district
  made their way to him,

and as they were baptized by him in the river Jordan
    they confessed their sins.
But when he saw a number of Pharisees
    and Sadducees coming for baptism he said to them,
    "Brood of vipers,
    who warned you to fly from the retribution that is coming?
But if you are repentant, produce the appropriate fruit,
    and do not presume to tell yourselves,
    'We have Abraham for our father,' because, I tell you,
    God can raise children for Abraham from these stones.
Even now the axe is laid to the roots of the trees,
    so that any tree which fails to produce good fruit
    will be cut down and thrown on the fire.
I baptize you in water for repentance,
    but the one who follows me is more powerful than I am,
    and I am not fit to carry his sandals;
    he will baptize you with the Holy Spirit and fire.
His winnowing-fan is in his hand;
    he will clear his threshing-floor
    and gather his wheat into the barn;
    but the chaff he will burn in a fire that will never go out."
This is the gospel of the Lord.

177. Matthew 4:12-17   Repent, for the kingdom of heaven is
close at hand.

+ A reading from the holy gospel according to Matthew
Hearing that John has been arrested [Jesus] went back to Galilee,
    and leaving Nazareth he went and settled in Capernaum,
    a lakeside town on the borders of Zebulun and Naphtali.
In this way the prophecy of Isaiah was to be fulfilled:

Land of Zebulun! Land of Naphtali!
Way of the sea on the far side of Jordan,
Galilee of the nations!
The people that lived in darkness
has seen a great light;
on those who dwell in the land and shadow of death
a light has dawned.

From that moment Jesus began his preaching with the message,
    "Repent, for the kingdom of heaven is close at hand."
This is the gospel of the Lord.

178. Matthew 5:1-12   When he saw the crowds, he went up to the hill and taught his disciples.

✝ A reading from the holy gospel according to Matthew
Seeing the crowds, [Jesus] went up the hill.
There he sat down and was joined by his disciples.
Then he began to speak. This is what he taught them:

"How happy are the poor in spirit;
theirs is the kingdom of heaven.
Happy the gentle:
they shall have the earth for their heritage.
Happy those who mourn:
they shall be comforted.
Happy those who hunger and thirst for what is right:
they shall be satisfied.
Happy the merciful:
they shall have mercy shown them.
Happy the pure in heart:
they shall see God.
Happy the peacemakers:
they shall be called sons of God.
Happy those who are persecuted in the cause of right:
theirs is the kingdom of heaven.

"Happy are you when people abuse you and persecute you
and speak all kinds of calumny against you on my account.
Rejoice and be glad, for your reward will be great in heaven;
this is how they persecuted the prophets before you."
This is the gospel of the Lord.

179. Matthew 5:13-16   Let your light shine before men.

✝ A reading from the holy gospel according to Matthew
Jesus said to his disciples:
"You are the salt of the earth.
But if salt becomes tasteless, what can make it salty again?
It is good for nothing,
and can only be thrown out
to be trampled underfoot by men.

"You are the light of the world.
A city built on a hill-top cannot be hidden.
No one lights a lamp to put it under a tub;
they put it on the lamp-stand

where it shines for everyone in the house.
In the same way your light must shine in the sight of men,
    so that, seeing your good works,
    they may give the praise to your Father in heaven."
This is the gospel of the Lord.

180. Matthew 5:17-47   But I am speaking to you.

✝ A reading from the holy gospel according to Matthew
Jesus said to his disciples:
"Do not imagine that I have come
    to abolish the Law or the Prophets.
I have come not to abolish but to complete them.
I tell you solemnly, till heaven and earth disappear,
    not one dot, not one little stroke,
    shall disappear from the Law until its purpose is achieved.
Therefore, the man who infringes even one of the least
    of these commandments and teaches others to do the same
    will be considered the least in the kingdom of heaven;
    but the man who keeps them and teaches them
    will be considered great in the kingdom of heaven.

"For I tell you, if your virtue goes no deeper
    than that of the scribes and Pharisees,
    you will never get into the kingdom of heaven.

"You have learned how it was said to our ancestors:
    You must not kill;
    and if anyone does kill
    he must answer for it before the court.
But I say this to you:
    anyone who is angry with his brother
    will answer for it before the court;
    if a man calls his brother 'Fool'
    he will answer for it before the Sanhedrin;
    and if a man calls him 'Renegade'
    he will answer for it in hell fire.
So then, if you are bringing your offering to the altar
    and there remember
    that your brother has something against you,
    leave your offering there before the altar,
    go and be reconciled with your brother first,
    and then come back and present your offering.

Come to terms with your opponent in good time
    while you are still on the way to the court with him,
    or he may hand you over to the judge
    and the judge to the officer,
    and you will be thrown into prison.
I tell you solemnly,
    you will not get out till you have paid the last penny.

"You have learned how it was said: You must not commit adultery.
But I say this to you: if a man looks at a woman lustfully,
    he has already committed adultery with her in his heart.
If your right eye should cause you to sin,
    tear it out and throw it away;
    for it will do you less harm to lose one part of you
    than to have your whole body thrown into hell.
And if your right hand should cause you to sin,
    cut it off and throw it away;
    for it will do you less harm to lose one part of you
    than to have your whole body go to hell.

"It has also been said:
    Anyone who divorces his wife
    must give her a writ of dismissal.
But I say this to you: everyone who divorces his wife,
    except for the case of fornication, makes her an adulteress;
    and anyone who marries a divorced woman
    commits adultery.

"Again, you have learned how it was said to our ancestors:
    You must not break your oath,
    but must fulfill your oaths to the Lord.
But I say this to you: do not swear at all,
    either by heaven, since that is God's throne;
    or by the earth, since that is his footstool;
    or by Jerusalem, since that is the city of the great king.
Do not swear by your own head either,
    since you cannot turn a single hair white or black.
All you need say is 'Yes' if you mean yes,
    'No' if you mean no;
    anything more than this comes from the evil one.

"You have learned how it was said:
    Eye for eye and tooth for tooth.

But I say this to you: offer the wicked man no resistance.
On the contrary, if anyone hits you on the right cheek,
    offer him the other as well;
    if a man takes you to law and would have your tunic,
    let him have your cloak as well.
And if anyone orders you to go one mile,
    go two miles with him.
Give to anyone who asks, and if anyone wants to borrow,
    do not turn away.

"You have learned how it was said:
    You must love your neighbor and hate your enemy.
But I say this to you: love your enemies
    and pray for those who persecute you;
    in this way you will be sons of your Father in heaven,
    for he causes his sun to rise on bad men as well as good,
    and his rain to fall on honest and dishonest men alike.
For if you love those who love you,
    what right have you to claim any credit?
Even the tax collectors do as much, do they not?
And if you save your greetings for your brothers,
    are you doing anything exceptional?
Even the pagans do as much, do they not?"
This is the gospel of the Lord.

181. Matthew 9:1-8   Have confidence, my son, your sins are
forgiven.

✝ A reading from the holy gospel according to Matthew
[Jesus] got back in the boat, crossed the water
    and came to his own town.
Then some people appeared,
    bringing him a paralytic stretched out on a bed.
Seeing their faith, Jesus said to the paralytic,
    "Courage, my child, your sins are forgiven."
And at this some scribes said to themselves,
    "This man is blaspheming."
Knowing what was in their minds Jesus said,
    "Why do you have such wicked thoughts in your hearts?
Now, which of these is easier: to say,
    'Your sins are forgiven', or to say, 'Get up and walk'?
But to prove to you that the Son of Man

has authority on earth to forgive sins,"—
   he said to the paralytic—
   "Get up, and pick up your bed and go off home."
And the man got up and went home.
A feeling of awe came over the crowd when they saw this,
   and they praised God for giving such power to men.
   This is the gospel of the Lord.

182. Matthew 9:9-13   I did not come to call the just, but
sinners.

✝ A reading from the holy gospel according to Matthew
As Jesus was walking on from there
   he saw a man named Matthew sitting by the customs house,
   and he said to him, "Follow me."
And he got up and followed him.

While he was at dinner in the house
   it happened that a number of tax collectors and sinners
   came to sit at the table with Jesus and his disciples.
When the Pharisees saw this, they said to his disciples,
   "Why does your master eat with tax collectors and sinners?"
When he heard this he replied,
   "It is not the healthy who need the doctor, but the sick.
Go and learn the meaning of the words:
   What I want is mercy, not sacrifice.
And indeed I did not come to call the virtuous, but sinners."
This is the gospel of the Lord.

183. Matthew 18:15-20   You have won back your brother.

✝ A reading from the holy gospel according to Matthew
Jesus said to his disciples:
"If your brother does something wrong,
   go and have it out with him alone,
   between your two selves.
If he listens to you, you have won back your brother.
If he does not listen, take one or two others along with you:
   the evidence of two or three witnesses is required
   to sustain any charge.
But if he refuses to listen to these, report it to the community;
   and if he refuses to listen to the community,
   treat him like a pagan or a tax collector.

"I tell you solemnly,
    whatever you bind on earth
    shall be considered bound in heaven;
    whatever you loose on earth
    shall be considered loosed in heaven.

"I tell you solemnly once again,
    if two of you on earth agree to ask anything at all,
    it will be granted to you by my Father in heaven.
For where two or three meet in my name,
    I shall be there with them."
    This is the gospel of the Lord.

184. Matthew 18:21-35   This is the way my heavenly Father will deal with you unless each one forgives his brother from his heart.

✛ A reading from the holy gospel according to Matthew
Then Peter went up to [Jesus] and said,
    "Lord, how often must I forgive my brother if he wrongs me?
As often as seven times?"
Jesus answered,
    "Not seven, I tell you, but seventy-seven times.

"And so the kingdom of heaven may be compared to a king
    who decided to settle his accounts with his servants.
When the reckoning began,
    they brought him a man who owed ten thousand talents;
    but he had no means of paying,
    so his master gave orders that he should be sold,
    together with his wife and children and all his possessions,
    to meet the debt.
At this, the servant threw himself down at his master's feet.
    'Give me time,' he said, 'and I will pay the whole sum.'
And the servant's master felt so sorry for him
    that he let him go and cancelled the debt.
Now as this servant went out, he happened to meet
    a fellow servant who owed him one hundred denarii;
    and he seized him by the throat and began to throttle him.
'Pay what you owe me,' he said.
His fellow servant fell at his feet and implored him, saying,
    'Give me time and I will pay you.'
But the other would not agree;

on the contrary, he had him thrown into prison
    till he should pay the debt.
His fellow servants were deeply distressed
    when they saw what had happened,
    and they went to their master
    and reported the whole affair to him.
Then the master sent for him.
'You wicked servant,' he said,
    'I cancelled all that debt of yours when you appealed to me.
Were you not bound, then,
    to have pity on your fellow servant just as I had pity on you?'
And in his anger the master handed him over to the torturers
    till he should pay all his debt.
And that is how my heavenly Father will deal with you
    unless you each forgive your brother from your heart."
    This is the gospel of the Lord.

185. Matthew 25:31-46   Whatever you have done to the very
least of my brothers, you have done to me.

✝ A reading from the holy gospel according to Matthew
Jesus said:
"When the Son of Man comes in his glory,
    escorted by all the angels,
    then he will take his seat on his throne of glory.
All the nations will be assembled before him
    and he will separate men one from another
    as the shepherd separates sheep from goats.
He will place the sheep on his right hand
    and the goats on his left.
Then the King will say to those on his right hand,
    'Come, you whom my Father has blessed,
    take for your heritage the kingdom prepared for you
    since the foundation of the world.
For I was hungry and you gave me food;
    I was thirsty and you gave me drink;
    I was a stranger and you made me welcome;
    naked and you clothed me, sick and you visited me,
    in prison and you came to see me.'
Then the virtuous will say to him in reply,
    'Lord, when did we see you hungry and feed you;
    or thirsty and give you drink?

When did we see you a stranger and make you welcome;
  naked and clothe you;
  sick or in prison and go to see you?'
And the King will answer,
  'I tell you solemnly, in so far as you did this
  to one of the least of these brothers of mine,
  you did it to me.' Next he will say to those on his left hand,
  'Go away from me, with your curse upon you,
  to the eternal fire prepared for the devil and his angels.
For I was hungry and you never gave me food;
  I was thirsty and you never gave me anything to drink;
  I was a stranger and you never made me welcome,
  naked and you never clothed me,
  sick and you never visited me.'
Then it will be their turn to ask,
  'Lord, when did we see you hungry or thirsty,
  a stranger or naked, sick or in prison,
  and did not come to your help?'
Then he will answer,
  'I tell you solemnly, in so far as you neglected to do this
  to one of the least of these, you neglected to do it to me.'
And they will go away to eternal punishment,
  and the virtuous to eternal life."
  This is the gospel of the Lord.

186. Matthew 26:69-75   Peter went outside and wept bitterly.

✝ A reading from the holy gospel according to Matthew
Meanwhile Peter was sitting outside in the courtyard,
  and a servant-girl came up to him and said,
  "You too were with Jesus the Galilean."
But he denied it in front of them all.
"I do not know what you are talking about," he said.
When he went out to the gateway
  another servant-girl saw him and said to the people there,
  "This man was with Jesus the Nazarene."
And again, with an oath, he denied it,
  "I do not know the man."
A little later the bystanders came up and said to Peter,
  "You are one of them for sure!
Why, your accent gives you away."
Then he started calling down curses on himself and swearing,

"I do not know the man."
At that moment the cock crew,
  and Peter remembered what Jesus had said,
  "Before the cock crows
  you will have disowned me three times."
And he went outside and wept bitterly.
This is the gospel of the Lord.

187. Mark 12:28-34   This is the first commandment.

✝ A reading from the holy gospel according to Mark
One of the scribes who had listened to them debating
  and had observed how well Jesus had answered them,
  now came up and put a question to him,
  "Which is the first of all the commandments?"
Jesus replied, "This is the first:
  Listen, Israel, the Lord our God is the one Lord
  and you must love the Lord your God
  with all your heart, with all your soul,
  with all your mind and with all your strength.
The second is this: You must love your neighbor as yourself.
There is no commandment greater than these."
The scribe said to him, "Well spoken, Master;
  what you have said is true: that he is one and there is no other.
To love him with all your heart,
  with all your understanding and strength,
  and to love your neighbor as yourself,
  this is far more important than any holocaust or sacrifice."
Jesus, seeing how wisely he had spoken, said,
  "You are not far from the kingdom of God."
And after that no one dared to question him any more.
This is the gospel of the Lord.

188. Luke 7:36-50   Her many sins must have been forgiven
her, because she loved much.

✝ A reading from the holy gospel according to Luke
One of the Pharisees invited [Jesus] to a meal.
When he arrived at the Pharisee's house
  and took his place at table,

a woman came in, who had a bad name in the town.
She had heard he was dining with the Pharisee
　　and had brought with her an alabaster jar of ointment.
She waited behind him at his feet, weeping,
　　and her tears fell on his feet,
　　and she wiped them away with her hair;
　　then she covered his feet with kisses
　　and anointed them with the ointment.

When the Pharisee who had invited him saw this,
　　he said to himself, "If this man were a prophet,
　　he would know who this woman is that is touching him
　　and what a bad name she has."
Then Jesus took him up and said,
　　"Simon, I have something to say to you."
"Speak, Master," was the reply.
"There was once a creditor who had two men in his debt;
　　one owed him five hundred denarii, the other fifty.
They were unable to pay, so he pardoned them both.
Which of them will love him more?"
"The one who was pardoned more, I suppose," answered Simon.
Jesus said, "You are right."

Then he turned to the woman.
"Simon," he said, "you see this woman?
I came into your house, and you poured no water over my feet,
　　but she has poured out her tears over my feet
　　and wiped them away with her hair.
You gave me no kiss,
　　but she has been covering my feet with kisses
　　ever since I came in.
You did not anoint my head with oil,
　　but she has anointed my feet with ointment.
For this reason I tell you that her sins, her many sins,
　　must have been forgiven her,
　　or she would not have shown such great love.
It is the man who is forgiven little who shows little love."
Then he said to her, "Your sins are forgiven."
Those who were with him at table began to say to themselves,
　　"Who is this man, that he even forgives sins?"
But he said to the woman, "Your faith has saved you; go in peace."
This is the gospel of the Lord.

189. Luke 13:1-5   Unless you repent you will all perish as they did.

✝ A reading from the holy gospel according to Luke
It was just about this time that some people arrived
    and told [Jesus] about the Galileans
    whose blood Pilate had mingled with that of their sacrifices.
At this he said to them,
    "Do you suppose these Galileans who suffered like that
    were greater sinners than any other Galileans?
They were not, I tell you.
No; but unless you repent you will all perish as they did.
Or those eighteen
    on whom the tower at Siloam fell and killed them?
Do you suppose that they were more guilty
    than all the other people living in Jerusalem?
They were not, I tell you.
No; but unless you repent you will all perish as they did."
This is the gospel of the Lord.

190. Luke 15:1-10   Heaven is filled with joy when one sinner turns back to God.

✝ A reading from the holy gospel according to Luke
The tax collectors and the sinners, meanwhile,
    were all seeking his company to hear what [Jesus] had to say,
    and the Pharisees and the scribes complained.
"This man," they said, "welcomes sinners and eats with them."
So he spoke this parable to them:

"What man among you with a hundred sheep,
    losing one, would not leave the ninety-nine in the wilderness
    and go after the missing one till he found it?
And when he found it,
    would he not joyfully take it on his shoulders and then,
    when he got home, call together his friends and neighbors?
'Rejoice with me,' he would say,
    'I have found my sheep that was lost.'
In the same way, I tell you, there will be more rejoicing
    in heaven over one repentant sinner
    than over ninety-nine virtuous men
    who have no need of repentance.

"Or again, what woman with ten drachmas would not,

if she lost one, light a lamp and sweep out the house
   and search thoroughly till she found it?
And then, when she had found it,
   call together her friends and neighbors?
'Rejoice with me,' he would say,
   'I have found the drachma I lost.'
In the same way, I tell you, there is rejoicing
   among the angels of God over one repentant sinner."
   This is the gospel of the Lord.

191. Luke 15:11-32   When he was still far away, his father saw
him and was moved with mercy. He ran to him and embraced
and kissed him.

✛ A reading from the holy gospel according to Luke
[Jesus] also said, "A man had two sons.
The younger said to his father,
   'Father, let me have the share of the estate
   that would come to me.'
So the father divided the property between them.
A few days later, the younger son
   got together everything he had and left for a distant country
   where he squandered his money on a life of debauchery.

"When he had spent it all,
   that country experienced a severe famine,
   and now he began to feel the pinch,
   so he hired himself out to one of the local inhabitants
   who put him on his farm to feed the pigs.
And he would willingly have filled his belly
   with the husks the pigs were eating
   but no one offered him anything.
Then he came to his senses and said,
   'How many of my father's paid servants have more food
   than they want, and here am I dying of hunger!
I will leave this place and go to my father and say:
   Father, I have sinned against heaven and against you;
   I no longer deserve to be called your son;
   treat me as one of your paid servants.'
So he left the place and went back to his father.

"While he was still a long way off,
   his father saw him and was moved with pity.

He ran to the boy,
  clasped him in his arms and kissed him tenderly.
Then his son said,
  'Father, I have sinned against heaven and against you.
I no longer deserve to be called your son.'
But the father said to his servants, 'Quick!
Bring out the best robe and put it on him;
  put a ring on his finger and sandals on his feet.
Bring the calf we have been fattening, and kill it;
  we are going to have a feast, a celebration,
    because this son of mine was dead and has come back to life;
  he was lost and is found.' And they began to celebrate.

"Now the elder son was out in the fields, and on his way back,
  as he drew near the house, he could hear music and dancing.
Calling one of the servants he asked what it was all about.
'Your brother has come,' replied the servant,
  'and your father has killed the calf we had fattened
  because he has got him back safe and sound.'
He was angry then and refused to go in,
  and his father came out to plead with him;
  but he answered his father,
  'Look, all these years I have slaved for you
  and never once disobeyed your orders,
  yet you never offered me so much as a kid
  for me to celebrate with my friends.
But, for this son of yours,
  when he comes back after swallowing up your property—
  he and his women—you kill the calf we had been fattening.'

"The father said,
  'My son, you are with me always and all I have is yours.
But it was only right we should celebrate and rejoice,
  because your brother here was dead and has come to life;
  he was lost and is found.' "
  This is the gospel of the Lord.

192. Luke 17:1-4   If your brother sins against you seven times a day and returns to you seven times a day and says I am sorry, you must forgive him.

+ A reading from the holy gospel according to Luke
[Jesus] said to his disciples,

"Obstacles are sure to come,
  but alas for the one who provides them!
It would be better for him to be thrown into the sea
  with a millstone put round his neck
  than that he should lead astray a single one
  of these little ones.
Watch yourselves!

"If your brother does something wrong,
  reprove him and, if he is sorry, forgive him.
And if he wrongs you seven times a day
  and seven times comes back to you and says, 'I am sorry,'
  you must forgive him."
  This is the gospel of the Lord.

193. Luke 18:9-14 God, be merciful to me, a sinner.

✝ A reading from the holy gospel according to Luke
[Jesus] spoke the following parable to some people
  who prided themselves on being virtuous
  and despised everyone else.
"Two men went up to the Temple to pray,
  one a Pharisee, the other a tax collector.
The Pharisee stood there and said this prayer to himself,
  'I thank you, God, that I am not
  grasping, unjust, adulterous like the rest of mankind,
  and particularly that I am not like this tax collector here.
I fast twice a week; I pay tithes on all I get.'
The tax collector stood some distance away,
  not daring even to raise his eyes to heaven;
  but he beat his breast and said,
  'God be merciful to me, a sinner.'
This man, I tell you, went home again at rights with God;
  the other did not.
For everyone who exalts himself will be humbled,
  but the man who humbles himself will be exalted."
  This is the gospel of the Lord.

194. Luke 19:1-10 The Son of Man has come to seek out and
save what was lost.

✝ A reading from the holy gospel according to Luke
[Jesus] entered Jericho and was going through the town

when a man whose name was Zacchaeus
made his appearance;
he was one of the senior tax collectors and a wealthy man.
He was anxious to see what kind of man Jesus was,
  but he was too short and could not see him for the crowd;
  so he ran ahead and climbed a sycamore tree
  to catch a glimpse of Jesus who was to pass that way.
When Jesus reached the spot he looked up and spoke to him:
  "Zacchaeus, come down.
Hurry, because I must stay at your house today."
And he hurried down and welcomed him joyfully.
They all complained when they saw what was happening.
"He has gone to stay at a sinner's house," they said.
But Zacchaeus stood his ground and said to the Lord,
  "Look, sir,
  I am going to give half my property to the poor,
  and if I have cheated anybody
  I will pay him back four times the amount."
And Jesus said to him,
  "Today salvation has come to this house,
  because this man too is a son of Abraham;
  for the Son of Man has come to seek out
  and save what was lost."
  This is the gospel of the Lord.

195. Luke 23:39-43   Today you will be with me in paradise.

✠ A reading from the holy gospel according to Luke
One of the criminals hanging there abused him.
"Are you not the Christ?" he said.
"Save yourself and us as well."
But the other spoke up and rebuked him,
  "Have you no fear of God at all?" he said.
"You got the same sentence as he did,
  but in our case we deserved it:
  we are paying for what we did.
But this man has done nothing wrong.
Jesus," he said,
  "remember me when you come into your kingdom."
"Indeed, I promise you," he replied,
  "today you will be with me in paradise."
  This is the gospel of the Lord.

196. John 8:1-11   Go and sin no more.

☩ A reading from the holy gospel according to John
Jesus went to the Mount of Olives.

At daybreak he appeared in the Temple again;
    and as all the people came to him,
    he sat down and began to teach them.

The scribes and Pharisees brought a woman along
    who had been caught committing adultery;
    and making her stand there in full view of everybody,
    they said to Jesus, "Master,
    this woman was caught in the very act of committing adultery,
    and Moses has ordered us in the Law
    to condemn women like this to death by stoning.
What have you to say?"
They asked him this as a test,
    looking for something to use against him.
But Jesus bent down
    and started writing on the ground with his finger.
    As they persisted with their question,
    he looked up and said,
    "If there is one of you who has not sinned,
    let him be the first to throw a stone at her."
Then he bent down and wrote on the ground again.
When they heard this they went away one by one,
    beginning with the eldest,
    until Jesus was left alone with the woman,
    who remained standing there.
He looked up and said, "Woman, where are they?
Has no one condemned you?"
"No one, sir," she replied.
"Neither do I condemn you," said Jesus,
    "go away, and don't sin any more."
    This is the gospel of the Lord.

197. John 8:31-36   Everyone who commits sin is a slave of sin.

☩ A reading from the holy gospel according to John
To the Jews who believed in him Jesus said:

    "If you make my word your home
    you will indeed be my disciples,

you will learn the truth
and the truth will make you free."

They answered, "We are descended from Abraham
and we have never been the slaves of anyone;
what do you mean, 'You will be made free'?"
Jesus replied:

"I tell you most solemnly,
everyone who commits sin is a slave.
Now the slave's place in the house is not assured,
but the son's place is assured.
So if the Son makes you free,
you will be free indeed."
This is the gospel of the Lord.

198. John 15:1-8   The Father prunes every barren branch, and
every branch that bears fruit he makes it bear even more.

✝ A reading from the holy gospel according to John
Jesus said:

"I am the true vine,
and my Father is the vinedresser.
Every branch in me that bears no fruit
he cuts away,
and every branch that does bear fruit he prunes
to make it bear even more.
You are pruned already,
by means of the word that I have spoken to you.
Make your home in me, as I make mine in you.
As a branch cannot bear fruit all by itself,
but must remain part of the vine,
neither can you unless you remain in me.
I am the vine,
you are the branches.
Whoever remains in me, with me in him,
bears fruit in plenty;
for cut off from me you can do nothing.
Anyone who does not remain in me
is like a branch that has been thrown away
—he withers;
these branches are collected and thrown on the fire,
and they are burned.

If you remain in me
and my words remain in you,
you may ask what you will
and you shall get it.
It is to the glory of my Father that you should bear much fruit,
and then you will be my disciples."
This is the gospel of the Lord.

199. John 15:9-14   You are my friends if you do what I command you.

✢ A reading from the holy gospel according to John
Jesus said:

"As the Father has loved me,
so I have loved you.
Remain in my love,
If you keep my commandments
you will remain in my love,
just as I have kept my Father's commandments
and remain in his love.
I have told you this
so that my own joy may be in you
and your joy be complete.
This is my commandment:
love one another,
as I have loved you.
A man can have no greater love
than to lay down his life for his friends.
You are my friends,
if you do what I command you."
This is the gospel of the Lord.

200. John 19:13-37   They shall look upon him whom they pierced.

✢ A reading from the holy gospel according to John
Pilate had Jesus brought out,
    and seated himself on the chair of judgment
    at a place called the Pavement, in Hebrew Gabbatha.
It was Passover Preparation Day, about the sixth hour.
"Here is your king," said Pilate to the Jews.

"Take him away, take him away!" they said.
"Crucify him!"
"Do you want me to crucify your king?" said Pilate.
The chief priests answered, "We have no king except Caesar."
So in the end Pilate handed him over to them to be crucified.

They then took charge of Jesus, and carrying his own cross
   he went out of the city to the place of the skull or,
   as it was called in Hebrew, Golgotha,
   where they crucified him with two others,
   one on either side with Jesus in the middle.
Pilate wrote out a notice and had it fixed to the cross;
   it ran: "Jesus the Nazarene, King of the Jews."
This notice was read by many of the Jews,
   because the place where Jesus was crucified
   was not far from the city,
   and the writing was in Hebrew, Latin and Greek.
So the Jewish chief priests said to Pilate,
   "You should not write 'King of the Jews,'
   but 'This man said: I am King of the Jews.' "
Pilate answered, "What I have written, I have written."

When the soldiers had finished crucifying Jesus
   they took his clothing and divided it into four shares,
   one for each soldier.
His undergarment was seamless,
   woven in one piece from neck to hem;
   so they said to one another,
   "Instead of tearing it,
   let's throw dice to decide who is to have it."
In this way the words of scripture were fulfilled:
   They shared out my clothing among them.
   They cast lots for my clothes.
This is exactly what the soldiers did.

Near the cross of Jesus stood his mother and his mother's sister,
   Mary the wife of Clopas, and Mary of Magdala.
Seeing his mother
   and the disciple he loved standing near her,
   Jesus said to his mother, "Woman, this is your son."
Then to the disciple he said, "This is your mother."
And from that moment
   the disciple made a place for her in his home.

After this,
  Jesus knew that everything had now been completed,
  and to fulfill the scripture perfectly he said:

"I am thirsty."

A jar full of vinegar stood there,
  so putting a sponge soaked in the vinegar
  on a hyssop stick they held it up to his mouth.
After Jesus had taken the vinegar he said,
  "It is accomplished";
  and bowing his head he gave up his spirit.

It was Preparation Day, and to prevent the bodies
  remaining on the cross during the sabbath—
since that sabbath was a day of special solemnity—
  the Jews asked Pilate to have the legs broken
  and the bodies taken away.
Consequently the soldiers came and broke the legs
  of the first man who had been crucified with him
  and then of the other.
When they came to Jesus, they found he was already dead,
  and so instead of breaking his legs
  one of the soldiers pierced his side with a lance;
  and immediately there came out blood and water.
This is the evidence of one who saw it—
  trustworthy evidence, and he knows he speaks the truth—
  and he gives it so that you may believe as well.
Because all this happened to fulfill the words of scripture:
  Not one bone of his will be broken;

and again, in another place scripture says:
  They will look on the one whom they have pierced.
  This is the gospel of the Lord.

201. John 20:19-23   Receive the Holy Spirit; whose sins you
forgive, they are forgiven.

✢ A reading from the holy gospel according to John
In the evening of that same day, the first day of the week,
  the doors were closed in the room where the disciples were,
  for fear of the Jews.
Jesus came and stood among them.
He said to them, "Peace be with you,"

and showed them his hands and his side.
The disciples were filled with joy when they saw the Lord,
and he said to them again, "Peace be with you."

"As the Father sent me,
so am I sending you."

After saying this he breathed on them and said:

"Receive the Holy Spirit.
For those whose sins you forgive,
they are forgiven;
for those whose sins you retain,
they are retained."
This is the gospel of the Lord.

INVITATION OF THE MINISTER FOR THE GENERAL CONFESSION OF SINS

202. If the prayer is directed to the Father:

1
Dear friends in Christ, our merciful Father does not
desire the death of the sinner but rather that he
should turn back to him and have life. Let us pray
that we who are sorry for our past sins may fear no
future evil and sin no more.
R̷. Spare us, Lord; spare your people.

2
God who is infintely merciful pardons all who are
repentant and takes away their guilt. Confident in his
goodness, let us ask him to forgive all our sins as we
confess them with sincerity of heart.
R̷. Lord, hear our prayer.

3
God gave us his Son for our sins and raised him up to
make us holy. Let us humbly pray to the Father.
R̷. Lord, have mercy on your people.

4
God our Father waits for the return of those who are
lost and welcomes them back as his children. Let us

pray that we may turn back to him and be received
with kindness into his house.
℞. Lord, do not hold our sins against us.

Or:

Father, we have sinned in your sight; we are unworthy to be called your children.

5

Our God seeks out what is lost, leads home the
abandoned, binds up what is broken and gives
strength to the weak; let us ask him to help us.
℞. Lord, heal our weakness.

203. If the prayer is directed to Christ:

1

Jesus Christ is the victor over sin and death: in his
mercy may he pardon our offenses against God and
reconcile us with the Church we have wounded by
our sins.
℞. Lord Jesus, be our salvation.

2

In his great love Christ willingly suffered and died
for our sins and for the sins of all mankind. Let us
come before him with faith and hope to pray for the
salvation of the world.
℞. Christ, graciously hear us.

3

Let us pray with confidence to Christ, the Good
Shepherd, who seeks out the lost sheep and carries it
back with joy.
℞. Lord, seek us out and bring us home.

4

Christ our Lord bore our sins upon the cross and by
his suffering has brought us healing, so that we live
for God and are dead to sin. Let us pray with humility
and trust.
℞. Lord, to whom shall we go? You have the words of

eternal life. We have come to believe and to know that you are the Christ, the Son of God.

Or:
Have pity on us, and help us.

5
Christ our Lord was given up to death for our sins and rose again for our justification. Let us pray to him with confidence in his goodness.
R̷. You are our Savior

Or:
Jesus Christ, Son of the living God, have pity on us.

PENITENTIAL INTERCESSIONS

(At least one of the intercessions should always be a petition for a true conversion of heart.)

204. If the prayer is addressed to the Father:

1
—By human weakness we have disfigured the holiness of the Church: pardon all our sins and restore us to full communion with our brethren.
R̷. Lord, hear our prayer. Or: Lord, hear us.

Or another suitable response may be used.

—Your mercy is our hope: welcome us to the sacrament of reconciliation. R̷.

—Give us the will to change our lives, and the lives of others, by charity, good example and prayer. R̷.

—As we make our confession, rescue us from slavery to sin and lead us to the freedom enjoyed by your children. R̷.

—Make us a living sign of your love for all to see: people reconciled with you and with each other. R̷.

—Through the sacrament of reconciliation may we

grow in your peace and seek to spread it throughout the world. ℟.

—In this sign of your love you forgive us our sins: may it teach us to love others and to forgive their sins against us. ℟.

—In your mercy clothe us in the wedding garment of grace and welcome us to your table. ℟.

—Forgive us our sins, lead us in the ways of goodness and love, and bring us to the reward of everlasting peace. ℟.

—Give light to our darkness and lead us by your truth. ℟.

—In justice you punish us: in your mercy set us free for the glory of your name. ℟.

—May your power keep safe from all danger those whom your love sets free from the chains of sin. ℟.

—Look on our weakness: do not be angry and condemn, but in your love cleanse, guide and save us. ℟.

—In your mercy free us from the past and enable us to begin a new life of holiness. ℟.

—When we stray from you, guide us back into the way of holiness, love and peace. ℟.

—By your redeeming love overcome our sinfulness and the harm it has brought us. ℟.

—Blot out the sins of the past and fit us for the life that is to come. ℟.

2

The following intercessions may be used with a variable response or with an invariable response as in the *Liturgy of the Hours*.

In your goodness, forgive our sins against the unity of your family,
—make us one in heart, one in spirit.

We have sinned, Lord, we have sinned,
—take away our sins by your saving grace.

Give us pardon for our sins,
—and reconciliation with your Church.

Touch our hearts and change our lives, make us grow
always in your friendship,
—help us to make up for our sins against your wisdom and goodness.

Cleanse and renew your Church, Lord,
—may it grow in strength as a witness to you.

Touch the hearts of those who have abandoned you
through sin and scandal,
—call them back to you and keep them faithful in
your love.

May we show forth in our lives the sufferings of your
Son,
—you raised us up to life when you raised him from
the dead.

Have mercy on us, Lord, as we praise and thank you,
—with your pardon give us also your peace.

Lord, our sins are many, but we trust in your mercy,
—call us, and we shall turn to you.

Receive us as we come before you with humble and
contrite hearts,
—those who trust in you shall never trust in vain.

We have turned away from you and fallen into sin,
—we have followed evil ways and rejected your
commandments.

Turn to us, Lord, and show us your mercy; blot out
our sins,
—cast them into the depths of the sea.

Restore us, Lord, to your favor, and give us joy in
your presence,
—may our glory be to serve you with all our hearts.

205. If the prayer is addressed to Christ:

1
Romans 5:10
—By your death you reconciled us with the Father
and brought us salvation.
℟. **Lord, have mercy.** Or: **Christ, hear us.**

Or another suitable response may be used.

Romans 8:34
—You died and rose again, and sit at the right hand of
the Father, to make intercession for us. ℟.

1 Corinthians 1:30
—You came from God as our wisdom and justice, our
sanctification and redemption. ℟.

1 Corinthians 6:11
—You washed mankind in the Spirit of our God; you
made us holy and righteous. ℟.

1 Corinthians 8:12
—You warned us that if we sin against each other we
sin against you. ℟.

2 Corinthians 8:9
—Though you were rich you became poor for our
sake, so that by your poverty we might become rich.
℟.

Galatians 1:4
—You gave yourself up for our sins to save us from
this evil world. ℟.

1 Thessalonians 1:10
—You rose from the dead to save us from the anger
that was to come. ℟.

1 Timothy 1:15
—You came into the world to save sinners. ℟.

1 Timothy 2:6
—You gave yourself up to bring redemption to all. ℟.

2 Timothy 1:10
—You destroyed death and gave light to life. ℟.

2 Timothy 4:1
—You will come to judge the living and the dead. ℟.

Titus 2:14
—You gave yourself up for us to redeem us from all sin and to prepare for yourself a holy people, marked as your own, devoted to good works. ℟.

Hebrews 2:17
—You showed us your mercy, and as a faithful high priest in the things of God you made atonement for the sins of the people. ℟.

Hebrews 5:9
—You became the source of salvation for all who obey you. ℟.

Hebrews 9:15
—Through the Holy Spirit you offered yourself to God as a spotless victim, cleansing our consciences from lifeless works. ℟.

Hebrews 9:28
—You were offered in sacrifice to undo the sins of the many. ℟.

1 Peter 3:18
—Once and for all you died for our sins, the innocent one for the guilty. ℟.

1 John 2:2
—You are the atonement for our sins and for the sins of the world. ℟.

John 3:16, 35
—You died that those who believe in you may not perish but have eternal life. ℟.

Matthew 18:11
—You came into the world to seek and save what was lost. ℟.

John 3:17
—You were sent by the Father, not to judge the world but to save it. ℟.

Mark 2:10
—You have power on earth to forgive sins. ℟.

Matthew 11:28
—You invite all who labor and are burdened to come to you to be refreshed. ℟.

Matthew 16:19, 18:18
—You gave your apostles the keys to the kingdom of heaven, the power to bind and to loose. ℟.

Matthew 22:38-40
—You told us that the whole law depends on love of God and of our neighbor. ℟.

John 10:10
—Jesus, life of all mankind, you came into the world to give us life, life in its fullness. ℟.

John 10:11
—Jesus, Good Shepherd, you gave your life for your sheep. ℟.

John 14:6; 8:32, 36
—Jesus, eternal truth, you give us true freedom. ℟.

John 14:6
—Jesus, you are the way to the Father. ℟.

John 11:25
—Jesus, you are the resurrection and life; those who believe in you, even if they are dead, will live. ℟.

John 15:1-2
—Jesus, true vine, the Father prunes your branches to make them bear even greater fruit. ℟.

2
The following intercessions may be used with a variable response or with an invariable response as in the *Liturgy of the Hours.*

Healer of the body and soul, bind up the wounds of our hearts,
—that our lives may grow strong through grace.

Help us to strip ourselves of sin,
—and put on the new life of grace.

Redeemer of the world, give us the spirit of penance
and a deeper devotion to your passion,
—so that we may have a fuller share in your risen
glory.

May your Mother, the refuge of sinners, intercede for
us,
—and ask you in your goodness to pardon our sins.

You forgave the woman who repented,
—show us also your mercy.

You brought back the lost sheep on your shoulders,
—pity us and lead us home.

You promised paradise to the good thief,
—take us with you into your Kingdom.

You died for us and rose again,
—make us share in your death and resurrection.

PROCLAMATION OF PRAISE
206.
Psalm 32:1-7, 10-11

R̷. **Rejoice in the Lord and sing for joy, friends of God.**

Happy the man whose offence is forgiven,
whose sin is remitted.
O happy the man to whom the Lord
imputes no guilt,
in whose spirit is no guile.   R̷.

I kept it secret and my frame was wasted,
I groaned all day long
for night and day your hand
was heavy upon me.
Indeed, my strength was dried up
as by the summer's heat.   R̷.

But now I have acknowledged my sins;
my guilt I did not hide.

I said: "I will confess
my offence to the Lord."
And you, Lord, have forgiven
the guilt of my sin.   R℘.

So let every good man pray to you
in the time of need.
The floods of water may reach high
but him they shall not reach.
You are my hiding place, O Lord;
you save me from distress.
You surround me with cries of deliverance.   R℘.

Many sorrows has the wicked
but he who trusts in the Lord,
loving mercy surrounds him.   R℘.

Rejoice, rejoice in the Lord,
exult, you just!
O come, ring out your joy,
all you upright of heart.   R℘.

Psalm 98: 1-9

R℘. **The Lord has remembered his mercy.**

Sing a new song to the Lord
for he has worked wonders.
His right hand and his holy arm
have brought salvation.   R℘.

The Lord has made known his salvation;
has shown his justice to the nations.
He has remembered his truth and love
for the house of Israel.   R℘.

All the ends of the earth have seen
the salvation of our God.
Shout to the Lord all the earth,
ring out your joy.   R℘.

Sing psalms to the Lord with the harp
with the sound of music.

With trumpets and the sound of the horn
acclaim the King, the Lord.
℟. The Lord has remembered his mercy.

Let the sea and all within it, thunder;
the world, and all its peoples.
Let the rivers clap their hands
and the hills ring out their joy
at the presence of the Lord, for he comes,
for he comes to rule the earth.
He will rule the world with justice
and the peoples with fairness.   ℟.

Psalm 100:2-5

℟. The Lord is loving and kind: his mercy is for ever.

Serve the Lord with gladness.
Come before him, singing for joy.   ℟.

Know that he, the Lord, is God.
He made us, we belong to him,
we are his people, the sheep of his flock.   ℟.

Go within his gates, giving thanks.
Enter his courts with songs of praise.
Give thanks to him and bless his name.   ℟.

Indeed, how good is the Lord,
eternal his merciful love.
He is faithful from age to age.   ℟.

Psalm 119:1, 10-13, 15-16, 18, 33, 105, 169, 170, 174-175.

℟. Blessed are you, Lord; teach me your decrees.

They are happy whose life is blameless,
who follow God's law!   ℟.

I have sought you with all my heart:
let me not stray from your commands.
I treasure your promise in my heart
lest I sin against you.   ℟.

Blessed are you, O Lord;
teach me your commands.
With my tongue I have recounted
the decrees of your lips.   R̸.

I will ponder all your precepts
and consider your paths.
I take delight in your commands;
I will not forget your word.   R̸.

Open my eyes that I may see
the wonders of your law.   R̸.

Teach me the demands of your precepts
and I will keep them to the end.   R̸.

Your word is a lamp for my steps
and a light for my path.   R̸.

Lord, let my cry come before you:
teach me by your word.   R̸.

Let my pleading come before you;
save me by your promise.
Lord, I long for your saving help
and your law is my delight.
Give life to my soul that I may praise you.
Let your decrees give me help.   R̸.

Psalm 103:1-4, 8-18

R̸. The mercy of the Lord is from everlasting to
everlasting on those who revere him.

My soul, give thanks to the Lord,
all my being, bless his holy name.
My soul, give thanks to the Lord
and never forget all his blessings.   R̸.

It is he who forgives all your guilt,
who heals every one of your ills,
who redeems your life from the grave,
who crowns you with love and compassion.   R̸.

The Lord is compassion and love,
slow to anger and rich in mercy.
His wrath will come to an end;
he will not be angry for ever.
He does not treat us according to our sins
nor repay us according to our faults.
℟. The mercy of the Lord is from everlasting to
everlasting on those who revere him.

For as the heavens are high above the earth
so strong is his love for those who fear him.
As far as the east is from the west
so far does he remove our sins.   ℟.

As a father has compassion on his sons,
the Lord has pity on those who fear him;
for he knows of what we are made,
he remembers that we are dust.   ℟.

As for man, his days are like grass;
he flowers like the flower of the field;
the wind blows and he is gone
and his place never sees him again.   ℟.

But the love of the Lord is everlasting
upon those who hold him in fear;
his justice reaches out to children's children
when they keep his covenant in truth,
when they keep his will in their mind.   ℟.

Psalm 145:1-21

℟. Day after day I will bless you, Lord: I will praise
your name for ever.

I will give you glory, O God my King,
I will bless your name for ever.   ℟.

I will bless you day after day
and praise your name for ever.
The Lord is great, highly to be praised,
his greatness cannot be measured.   ℟.

Age to age shall proclaim your works,
shall declare your mighty deeds,

shall speak of your splendor and glory,
tell the tale of your wonderful works.
They will speak of your terrible deeds,
recount your greatness and might.
They will recall your abundant goodness;
age to age shall ring out your justice. ℟.

The Lord is kind and full of compassion,
slow to anger, abounding in love.
How good is the Lord to all,
compassionate to all his creatures. ℟.

All your creatures shall thank you, O Lord,
and your friends shall repeat their blessing.
They shall speak of the glory of your reign
and declare your might, O God,
to make known to men your mighty deeds
and the glorious splendor of your reign.
Yours is an everlasting kingdom;
your rule lasts from age to age. ℟.

The Lord is faithful in all his words
and loving in all his deeds.
The Lord supports all who fall
and raises all who are bowed down. ℟.

The eyes of all creatures look to you
and you give them their food in due time.
You open wide your hand,
grant the desires of all who live. ℟.

The Lord is just in all his ways
and loving in all his deeds.
He is close to all who call him,
who call on him from their hearts. ℟.

He grants the desires of those who fear him,
he hears their cry and he saves them.
The Lord protects all who love him;
but the wicked he will utterly destroy. ℟.

Let me speak the praise of the Lord,
let all mankind bless his holy name
for ever, for ages unending. ℟.

Psalm 146:2-10

℟. **I will sing to my God all the days of my life.**

I will praise the Lord all my days,
make music to my God while I live.   ℟.

Put no trust in princes,
in mortal men in whom there is no help.
Take their breath, they return to clay
and their plans that day come to nothing.   ℟.

He is happy who is helped by Jacob's God,
whose hope is in the Lord his God,
who alone made heaven and earth,
the seas and all they contain.   ℟.

It is he who keeps faith for ever,
who is just to those who are oppressed.
It is he who gives bread to the hungry,
the Lord, who sets prisoners free,
the Lord who gives sight to the blind,
who raises up those who are bowed down,
the Lord, who protects the stranger
and upholds the widow and orphan.   ℟.

It is the Lord who loves the just
but thwarts the path of the wicked.
The Lord will reign for ever,
Sion's God, from age to age.   ℟.
Alleluia!

Isaiah 12:1b-6

℟. **Praise the Lord and call upon his name.**

You will say:
I give thanks to you, Lord,
you were angry with me
but your anger is appeased
and you have given me consolation.   ℟.

See now, he is the God of my salvation
I have trust now and no fear,

for the Lord is my strength, my song,
he is my salvation.
And you will draw water joyfully
from the springs of salvation. ℞.

That day, you will say:
Give thanks to the Lord,
call his name aloud.
Proclaim his deeds to the people,
declare his name sublime. ℞.

Sing of the Lord, for he has done marvelous things,
let them be made known to the whole world.
Cry out for joy and gladness,
you dwellers in Sion,
for great in the midst of you
is the Holy One of Israel. ℞.

Isaiah 61:10-11

℞. My spirit rejoices in my God.

I exult for joy in the Lord,
my soul rejoices in my God,
for he has clothed me in the garments of salvation,
he has wrapped me in the cloak of integrity,
like a bridegroom wearing his wreath,
like a bride adorned in her jewels. ℞.

For as the earth makes fresh things grow,
as a garden makes seeds spring up,
so will the Lord make both integrity and praise
spring up in the sight of the nations. ℞.

Jeremiah 31:10-14

℞. The Lord has redeemed his people.

Listen, nations, to the word of the Lord.
Tell this to the distant islands,
"He who scattered Israel gathers him,
he guards him as a shepherd guards his flock." ℞.

For the Lord has ransomed Jacob,
rescued him from a hand stronger than his own.
They will come and shout for joy on the heights of Zion,
they will throng toward the good things of the Lord:
corn and oil and wine,
sheep and oxen;
their soul will be like a watered garden,
they will sorrow no more.
℟. The Lord has redeemed his people.

The virgin will then take pleasure in the dance,
young men and old will be happy;
I will change their mourning into gladness,
comfort them, give them joy after their troubles,
refresh my priests with rich food,
and see my people have their fill of my good things
—it is the Lord who speaks.   ℟.

Daniel 3:52-57

℟. Bless the Lord, all the works of his hand: praise
and glorify him for ever.

May you be blessed, Lord, God of our ancestors,
be praised and extolled for ever.
Blessed be your glorious and holy name,
praised and extolled for ever.   ℟.

May you be blessed in the Temple of your sacred glory,
exalted and glorified above all else for ever:
blessed on the throne of your kingdom,
praised and exalted above all else for ever.   ℟.

Blessed, you fathomer of the great depths,
    enthroned on the cherubs,
praised and glorified above all else for ever;
blessed in the vault of heaven,
exalted and glorified above all else for ever.   ℟.

All things the Lord has made, bless the Lord:
give glory and eternal praise to him.   ℟.

Luke 1:46-55

℟. The Lord has remembered his mercy.

And Mary said:

My soul proclaims the greatness of the Lord,
my spirit rejoices in God my Savior
for he has looked with favor on his lowly servant. ℟.

From this day all generations will call me blessed:
the Almighty has done great things for me,
and holy is his Name. ℟.

He has mercy on those who fear him
in every generation. ℟.

He has shown the strength of his arm,
he has scattered the proud in their conceit. ℟.

He has cast down the mighty from their thrones,
and has lifted up the lowly. ℟.

He has filled the hungry with good things,
and the rich he has sent away empty. ℟.

He has come to the help of his servant Israel
for he has remembered his promise of mercy,
the promise he made to our fathers,
to Abraham and his children for ever. ℟.

Ephesians 1:3-10

℟. Blessed be God who chose us in Christ.

Blessed be God the Father of our Lord Jesus Christ,
who has blessed us with all the spiritual blessings of heaven in Christ. ℟.

Before the world was made, he chose us, chose us in Christ,
to be holy and spotless, and to live through love in his presence,
determining that we should become his adopted sons,
      through Jesus Christ for his own kind purposes,
to make us praise the glory of his grace,
his free gift to us in the Beloved,

in whom, through his blood, we gain our freedom,
the forgiveness of our sins.
Such is the richness of the grace
which he has showered on us
in all wisdom and insight.
℟. Blessed be God who chose us in Christ.

He has let us know the mystery of his purpose,
the hidden plan he so kindly made in Christ from the beginning
to act upon when the times had run their course to the end:
that he would bring everything together under Christ, as head,
everything in the heavens and everything on earth. ℟.

Revelation 15:3-4

℟. Great and wonderful are all your works, Lord.

How great and wonderful are all your works,
Lord God Almighty;
just and true are all your ways,
King of nations. ℟.

Who would not revere and praise your name, O Lord?
You alone are holy,
and all the pagans will come and adore you
for the many acts of justice you have shown. ℟.

CONCLUDING PRAYERS

207.

Father, all-powerful and ever-living God,
we do well always and everywhere to give you thanks.

When you punish us, you show your justice;
when you pardon us, you show your kindness;
yet always your mercy enfolds us.

When you chastise us, you do not wish to condemn us;
when you spare us, you give us time to make amends for our sins
through Christ our Lord.
℟. Amen.

208.
Lord God,
creator and ruler of your kingdom of light,
in your great love for this world
you gave up your only Son
for our salvation.
His cross has redeemed us,
his death has given us life,
his resurrection has raised us to glory.
Through him we ask you
to be always present among your family.
Teach us to be reverent in the presence of your glory;
fill our hearts with faith,
our days with good works,
our lives with your love;
may your truth be on our lips
and your wisdom in all our actions,
that we may receive the reward of everlasting life.

We ask this through Christ our Lord.
R℣. Amen.

209.
Lord Jesus Christ,
your loving forgiveness knows no limits.
You took our human nature
to give us an example of humility
and to make us faithful in every trial.
May we never lose the gifts you have given us,
but if we fall into sin
lift us up by your gift of repentance,
for you live and reign for ever and ever.
R℣. Amen.

210.
Father,
in your love you have brought us
from evil to good and from misery to happiness.
Through your blessings
give the courage of perseverance
to those you have called and justified by faith.

Grant this through Christ our Lord.
R̞. Amen.

211.
God and Father of us all,
you have forgiven our sins
and sent us your peace.
Help us to forgive each other
and to work together to establish peace in the world.

We ask this through Christ our Lord.
R̞. Amen.

212.
And may the blessing of almighty God,
the Father, and the Son, ✛ and the Holy Spirit,
come upon you and remain with you for ever.
R̞. Amen.

213.
May the Father bless us,
for we are his children, born to eternal life.
R̞. Amen.

May the Son show us his saving power,
for he died and rose for us.
R̞. Amen.

May the Spirit give us his gift of holiness
and lead us by the right path,
for he dwells in our hearts.
R̞. Amen.

214.
May the Father bless us,
for he has adopted us as his children.
R̞. Amen.

May the Son come to help us,
for he has received us as brothers and sisters.
R̞. Amen.

May the Spirit be with us,
for he has made us his dwelling place.
R̞. Amen.

APPENDIX I

ABSOLUTION FROM CENSURES

1. The form of absolution is not to be changed in respect to sins which are now reserved either in themselves or by reason of a censure. It is enough that the confessor intend to absolve the properly disposed penitent from these reserved sins. Until other provision is made and as may be necessary, the present regulations which make recourse to the competent authority obligatory are to be reserved. Before absolving from sins, however, the confessor may absolve from the censure, using the formula which is given below for absolution from censure outside the sacrament of penance.

2. When a priest, in accordance with the law, absolves a penitent from a censure outside the sacrament of penance, he uses the following formula:

By the power granted to me,
I absolve you
from the bond of excommunication (or suspension or
    interdict).
In the name of the Father, and of the Son, ✝
and of the Holy Spirit.
The penitent answers: **Amen.**

DISPENSATION FROM IRREGULARITY

3. When, in accordance with the law, a priest dispenses a penitent from an irregularity, either during confession, after absolution has been given, or outside the sacrament of penance, he says:

By the power granted to me
I dispense you from the irregularity
which you have incurred.
In the name of the Father, and of the Son, ✝
and of the Holy Spirit.
The penitent answers: **Amen.**

APPENDIX II

SAMPLE PENITENTIAL SERVICES

These services have been prepared by the Congregation for Divine Worship to help those who prepare or lead penitential celebrations.

PREPARING PENITENTIAL CELEBRATIONS

1. Penitential celebrations, mentioned in the *Rite of Penance* (nos. 36-37), are beneficial in fostering the spirit and virtue of penance among individuals and communities; they also help in preparing for a more fruitful celebration of the sacrament of penance. However, the faithful must be reminded of the difference between these celebrations and sacramental confession and absolution.[1]

2. The particular conditions of life, the manner of speaking, and the educational level of the congregation or special group should be taken into consideration. Thus liturgical commissions[2] and individual Christian communities preparing these celebrations should choose the texts and format most suited to the circumstances of each particular group.

3. To this end, several examples of penitential celebrations are given below. These are models and should be adapted to the specific conditions and needs of each community.

4. When the sacrament of penance is celebrated in these services, it follows the readings and homily, and the rite of reconciling several penitents with individual confession and absolution is used (nos. 54-59, *Rite of Penance*); when permitted by law, the rite for general confession and absolution is used (nos. 60-63, *Rite of Penance*).

I. PENITENTIAL CELEBRATIONS DURING LENT

5. Lent is the principal time of penance both for individual Christians and for the whole Church. It is therefore desira-

[1]See Congregation for the Doctrine of the Faith, *Normae pastorales circa absolutionem sacramentalem generali modo impertiendam,* June 16, 1972, no. X: *AAS* 64 (1972) 513.

[2]See Congregation of Rites, Instruction *Inter Oecumenici,* September 26, 1964, no. 39: *AAS* (1964) 110.

ble to prepare the Christian community for a fuller sharing in the paschal mystery by penitential celebrations during Lent.[1]

6. Texts from the lectionary and sacramentary may be used in these penitential celebrations; the penitential nature of the liturgy of the word in the Masses for Lent should be considered.

7. Two outlines of penitential celebrations suitable for Lent are given here. The first emphasizes penance as strengthening or restoring baptismal grace; the second shows penance as a preparation for a fuller sharing in the Easter mystery of Christ and his Church.

FIRST EXAMPLE

PENANCE LEADS TO A STRENGTHENING OF BAPTISMAL GRACE.

8. a) After an appropriate song and the greeting by the minister, the meaning of this celebration is explained to the people. It prepares the Christian community to recall their baptismal grace at the Easter Vigil and to reach newness of life in Christ through freedom from sins.

9. b) Prayer

My brothers and sisters, we have neglected the gifts of our baptism and fallen into sin. Let us ask God to renew his grace within us as we turn to him in repentance.

Let us kneel (or: Bow your heads before God).
All pray in silence for a brief period.
Let us stand (or: Raise your heads).

Lord Jesus,
you redeemed us by your passion
and raised us to new life in baptism.
Protect us with your unchanging love
and share with us the joy of your resurrection,
for you live and reign for ever and ever.
R⃫. Amen.

[1]See Second Vatican Council, constitution Sacrosanctum concilium, no. 109; Paul VI, Apostolic Constitution Paenitemini, February 17, 1966, no. IX: AAS 58 (1966) 185.

10. c) Readings

First Reading
1 Corinthians 10:1-13
All this that happened to the people of Moses in the desert
was written for our benefit.

A reading from the first letter of Paul to the Corinthians
I want to remind you, brothers,
  how our fathers were all guided by a cloud above them
  and how they all passed through the sea.
They were all baptized into Moses
  in this cloud and in this sea;
  all ate the same spiritual food
  and all drank the same spiritual drink,
  since they all drank from the spiritual rock
  that followed them as they went,
  and that rock was Christ.
In spite of this,
  most of them failed to please God
  and their corpses littered the desert.
These things all happened as warnings for us,
  not to have the wicked lusts
  for forbidden things that they had.
Do not become idolaters as some of them did,
  for scripture says: After sitting down to eat and drink,
  the people got up to amuse themselves.
We must never fall into sexual immorality:
  some of them did,
  and twenty-three thousand met their downfall
  in one day.
We are not to put the Lord to the test:
  some of them did, and they were killed by snakes.
You must never complain: some of them did,
  and they were killed by the Destroyer.
All this happened to them as a warning,
  and it was written down to be a lesson for us
  who are living at the end of the age.
The man who thinks he is safe must be careful
  that he does not fall.
The trials that you have had to bear
  are no more than people normally have.
You can trust God
  not to let you be tried beyond your strength,

and with any trial he will give you a way out of it
and the strength to bear it.
This is the Word of the Lord.

Responsorial Psalm
Psalm 106:6-10, 13-14, 19-22
R℣. (4): **Lord, remember us,
for the love you bear your people.**

**Then they cried to the Lord in their need
and he rescued them from their distress
and he led them along the right way,
to reach a city they could dwell in.** R℣.

**Let them thank the Lord for his love,
for the wonders he does for men.
For he satisfies the thirsty soul;
he fills the hungry with good things.** R℣.

**Some lay in darkness and in gloom,
prisoners in misery and chains,** R℣.

**Then they cried to the Lord in their need
and he rescued them from their distress.
He led them forth from darkness and gloom
and broke their chains to pieces.** R℣.

**Then they cried to the Lord in their need
and he rescued them from their distress.
He sent forth his word to heal them
and saved their life from the grave.** R℣.

**Let them thank the Lord for his love,
for the wonders he does for men.
Let them offer a sacrifice of thanks
and tell of his deeds with rejoicing.** R℣.

Gospel
Luke 15:4-7
Share my joy: I have found my lost sheep.

✝ A reading from the holy gospel according to Luke

**The tax collectors and the sinners, meanwhile,
were all seeking his company to hear what he had to say,
and the Pharisees and the scribes complained.**

"This man," they said,
"welcomes sinners and eats with them."
So he spoke this parable to them:

"What man among you with a hundred sheep,
    losing one,
    would not leave the ninety-nine in the wilderness
    and go after the missing one till he found it?
And when he found it,
    would he not joyfully take it on his shoulders and then,
    when he got home,
    call together his friends and neighbors?
'Rejoice with me,' he would say,
    'I have found my sheep that was lost.'
In the same way, I tell you,
    there will be more rejoicing in heaven
    over one repentant sinner
    than over ninety-nine virtuous men
    who have no need of repentance."
This is the gospel of the Lord.

or
Luke 15: 11-32
Your brother here was dead, and has come to life.

A reading from the holy gospel according to Luke

He also said, "A man had two sons.
The younger said to his father,
    'Father, let me have the share of the estate
    that would come to me.'
So the father divided the property between them.
A few days later,
    the younger son got together everything he had
    and left for a distant country
    where he squandered his money on a life of debauchery.
"When he had spent it all,
    that country experienced a severe famine,
    and now he began to feel the pinch,
    so he hired himself out to one of the local inhabitants
    who put him on his farm to feed the pigs.
And he would willingly have filled his belly
    with the husks the pigs were eating
    but no one offered him anything.
Then he came to his senses and said,
    'How many of my father's paid servants

have more food than they want,
and here am I dying of hunger!
I will leave this place and go to my father and say:
    Father, I have sinned against heaven and against you;
    I no longer deserve to be called your son;
    treat me as one of your paid servants.'
So he left the place and went back to his father.
While he was still a long way off,
    his father saw him and was moved with pity.
He ran to the boy
    clasped him in his arms and kissed him tenderly.
Then his son said,
    'Father, I have sinned against heaven and against you.
I no longer deserve to be called your son.'
But the father said to his servants,
    'Quick! Bring out the best robe and put it on him;
    put a ring on his finger and sandals on his feet.
Bring the calf we have been fattening, and kill it:
    we are going to have a feast, a celebration,
    because this son of mine was dead and has come back to life;
    he was lost and is found.'
And they began to celebrate.
"Now the elder son was out in the fields,
    and on his way back, as he drew near the house,
    he could hear music and dancing.
Calling one of the servants he asked what it was all about.
'Your brother has come,' replied the servant,
    'and your father has killed the calf we had fattened
    because he has got him back safe and sound.'
He was angry then and refused to go in,
    and his father came out to plead with him;
    but he answered his father,
    'Look, all these years I have slaved for you
    and never once disobeyed your orders,
    yet you never offered me so much as a kid
    for me to celebrate with my friends.
But, for this son of yours,
    when he comes back after swallowing up your property—
    he and his women—
    you kill the calf we had been fattening.
"The father said,
    'My son, you are with me always and all I have is yours.
But it was only right we should celebrate and rejoice,
    because your brother here was dead

and has come to life;
he was lost and is found.' "
This is the gospel of the Lord.

11. d) Homily
The celebrant may speak about:
—the need to fulfill the grace of baptism by living faithfully
the Gospel of Christ (see 1 Corinthians 10:1-13);
—the seriousness of sin committed after baptism (see Hebrews 6:4-8);
—the unlimited mercy of our God and Father who continually welcomes those who turn back to him after having sinned (see Luke 15);
—Easter as the feast when the Church rejoices over the Christian initiation of catechumens and the reconciliation of penitents.

12. e) Examination of conscience.
After the homily, the examination of conscience takes place;
a sample text is given in Appendix III, page 213. A period of silence should always be included so that each person may personally examine his conscience. In a special way the people should examine their conscience on the baptismal promises which will be renewed at the Easter Vigil.

13. f) Act of repentance
The deacon (or another minister, if there is no deacon) speaks to the assembly:

My brothers and sisters, the hour of God's favor draws near, the day of his mercy and of our salvation, when death was destroyed and eternal life began. This is the season for planting new vines in God's vineyard, the time for pruning the vines to ensure a richer harvest.

We all acknowledge that we are sinners. We are moved to penance, encouraged by the example and prayers of our brothers and sisters. We admit our guilt and say: "Lord, I acknowledge my sins; my offenses are always before me. Turn away your face, Lord, from my sins, and blot out all my wrong-doing. Give me back the joy of your salvation and give me a new and steadfast spirit."

We are sorry for having offended God by our sins.
May he be merciful and hear us as we ask to be
restored to his friendship and numbered among the
living who share the joy of Christ's risen life.

Then the priest sprinkles the congregation with holy water,
while all sing (say):

Cleanse us, Lord, from all our sins;
Wash us, and we shall be whiter than snow.

Then the priest says:
Lord our God,
you created us in love
and redeemed us in mercy.
While we were exiled from heaven
by the jealousy of the evil one,
you gave us your only Son,
who shed his blood to save us.
Send now your Holy Spirit
to breathe new life into your children,
for you do not want us to die
but to live for you alone.
You do not abandon those who abandon you;
correct us as a Father
and restore us to your family.

Lord,
your sons and daughters stand before you
in humility and trust.
Look with compassion on us
as we confess our sins.
Heal our wounds;
stretch out a hand of pity
to save us and raise us up.
Keep us free from harm
as members of Christ's body,
as sheep of your flock,
as children of your family.
Do not allow the enemy
to triumph over us
or death to claim us for ever,
for you raised us to new life in baptism.

Hear, Lord, the prayers we offer from contrite hearts.
Have pity on us as we acknowledge our sins.
Lead us back to the way of holiness.
Protect us now and always
from the wounds of sin.
May we ever keep safe in all its fullness
the gift your love once gave us
and your mercy now restores.

We ask this through our Lord Jesus Christ, your Son,
who lives and reigns with you and the Holy Spirit,
one God for ever and ever.
℟. Amen.

The celebration ends with an appropriate song and the
dismissal of the people.

SECOND EXAMPLE

PENANCE PREPARES FOR A FULLER SHARING
IN THE PASCHAL MYSTERY OF CHRIST FOR
THE SALVATION OF THE WORLD

14. a) After an appropriate song and the greeting by the
minister, the faithful are briefly reminded that they are
linked with each other in sin and in repentance so that each
should take his calling to conversion as an occasion of grace
for the whole community.

15. b) Prayer

My brothers and sisters, let us pray that by penance
we may be united with Christ, who was crucified for
our sins, and so share with all mankind in his resurrection.

Let us kneel (or: Bow your heads before God).
All pray in silence for a brief period.
Let us stand (or: Raise your heads).

Lord, our God and Father,
through the passion of your Son
you gave us new life.
By our practice of penance

make us one with him in his dying
so that we and all mankind
may be one with him
in his resurrection.

We ask this through Christ our Lord.
R⁊. Amen.

Or:

Almighty and merciful Father,
send your Holy Spirit
to inspire and strengthen us,
so that by always carrying
the death of Jesus in our bodies
we may also show forth the power of his risen life.

We ask this through Christ our Lord.
R⁊. Amen.

16. c) Readings

First Reading
Isaiah 53:1-7, 10-12
He is the one who bore our sufferings.

A reading from the book of the prophet Isaiah

"Who could believe what we had heard
and to whom has the power of the Lord been revealed?"
Like a sapling he grew up in front of us,
like a root in arid ground.
Without beauty, without majesty (we saw him),
no looks to attract our eyes;
a thing despised and rejected by men,
a man of sorrows and familiar with suffering,
a man to make people screen their faces;
he was despised and we took no account of him.

And yet ours were the sufferings he bore,
ours the sorrows he carried.
But we, we thought of him as someone punished,
struck by God, and brought low.
Yet he was pierced through for our faults,
crushed for our sins.
On him lies a punishment that brings us peace,
and through his wounds we are healed.

We had all gone astray like sheep,
each taking his own way,
and the Lord burdened him
with the sins of all of us.
Harshly dealt with, he bore it humbly,
he never opened his mouth,
like a lamb that is led to the slaughterhouse,
like a sheep that is dumb before its shearers
never opening its mouth.

The Lord has been pleased to crush him with suffering.
If he offers his life in atonement,
he shall see his heirs, he shall have a long life
and through him what the Lord wishes will be done.

His soul's anguish over
he shall see the light and be content.
By his suffering shall my servant justify many,
taking their faults on himself.

Hence I will grant whole hordes for his tribute,
he shall divide the spoil with the mighty,
for surrendering himself to death
and letting himself be taken for a sinner,
while he was bearing the faults of many
and praying all the time for sinners.
This is the Word of the Lord.

Responsorial Psalm
Psalm 22:2-3, 7-9, 18-28
R̞. Father, your will be done.
My God, my God, why have you forsaken me?
You are far from my plea and the cry of my distress.
O my God, I call by day and you give no reply;
I call by night and I find no peace. R̞.

But I am a worm and no man,
the butt of men, laughing-stock of the people.
All who see me deride me.
They curl their lips, they toss their heads.
'He trusted in the Lord, let him save him;
let him release him if this is his friend. R̞.

I can count every one of my bones.
These people stare at me and gloat;
they divide my clothing among them.
They cast lots for my robe. R̞.

O Lord, do not leave me alone,
my strength, make haste to help me!
Rescue my soul from the sword,
my life from the grip of these dogs.
Save my life from the jaws of these lions,
my poor soul from the horns of these oxen.   R̷.

I will tell of your name to my brethren
and praise you where they are assembled.
'You who fear the Lord give him praise;
all sons of Jacob, give him glory.
Revere him, Israel's sons.   R̷.

For he has never despised
nor scorned the poverty of the poor.
From him he has not hidden his face,
but he heard the poor man when he cried.'   R̷.

You are my praise in the great assembly.
My vows I will pay before those who fear him.
The poor shall eat and shall have their fill.
They shall praise the Lord, those who seek him.
May their hearts live for ever and ever!   R̷.

All the earth shall remember and return to the Lord,
all families of the nations worship before him.   R̷.

Second Reading
1 Peter 2:20-25
You had gone astray but now you have come back to the
shepherd and guardian of your souls.

A reading from the first letter of Peter

But there is nothing meritorious in taking a beating patiently
   if you have done something wrong to deserve it.
The merit, in the sight of God,
   is in bearing it patiently
   when you are punished after doing your duty.
This, in fact, is what you were called to do,
   because Christ suffered for you
   and left an example for you to follow the way he took.
He had not done anything wrong,
   and there had been no perjury in his mouth.
He was insulted and did not retaliate with insults;
   when he was tortured he made no threats
   but he put his trust in the righteous judge.
He was bearing our faults in his own body on the cross,

so that we might die to our faults and live for holiness;
through his wounds you have been healed.
You had gone astray like sheep
but now you have come back to the shepherd
and guardian of your souls.
This is the Word of the Lord.

Gospel
Verse before the gospel
**Glory to you, Lord; you were given up to death for
our sins and rose again for our justification. Glory to
you, Lord.**
Or an appropriate song may be sung.

Mark 10:32-45 (or short form: Mark 10:32-34, 42-45)
Now we are going up to Jerusalem, and the Son of Man will
be handed over.

+ A reading from the holy gospel according to Mark

**They were on the road, going up to Jerusalem;
Jesus was walking on ahead of them;
they were in a daze,
and those who followed were apprehensive.
Once more taking the Twelve aside
he began to tell them what was going to happen to him:
"Now we are going up to Jerusalem,
and the Son of Man is about to be handed over
to the chief priests and the scribes.
They will condemn him to death
and will hand him over to the pagans,
who will mock him and spit at him
and scourge him and put him to death;
and after three days he will rise again."
[James and John, the sons of Zebedee, approached him.
"Master," they said to him,
"we want you to do us a favor."
He said to them,
"What is it you want me to do for you?"
They said to him,
"Allow us to sit one at your right hand
and the other at your left in your glory."
"You do not know what you are asking,"
Jesus said to them.
"Can you drink the cup that I must drink,
or be baptized with the baptism**

with which I must be baptized?"
They replied, "We can."
Jesus said to them,
"The cup that I must drink you shall drink,
and with the baptism with which I must be baptized
you shall be baptized,
but as for seats at my right hand or my left,
these are not mine to grant;
they belong to those to whom they have been allotted."
When the other ten heard this
they began to feel indignant with James and John]
so Jesus called them to him and said to them,
"You know that among the pagans
their so-called rulers lord it over them,
and their great men make their authority felt.
This is not to happen among you.
No; anyone who wants to become great
among you must be your servant,
and anyone who wants to be first among you
must be slave to all.
For the Son of Man himself did not come
to be served but to serve,
and to give his life as a ransom for many."
This is the gospel of the Lord.

17. d) Homily
The celebrant may speak about:
—sin, by which we offend God and also Christ's body, the
Church, whose members we became in baptism;
—sin as a failure of love for Christ who in the paschal
mystery showed his love for us to the end;
—the way we affect each other when we do good or choose
evil;
—the mystery of vicarious satisfaction by which Christ bore
the burden of our sins, so that by his wounds we would be
healed (see Isaiah 53; 1 Peter 2:24);
—the social and ecclesial dimension of penance by which
individual Christians share in the work of converting the
whole community;
—the celebration of Easter as the feast of the Christian
community which is renewing itself by the conversion or
repentance of each member, so that the Church may become
a clearer sign of salvation in the world.

18. e) Examination of conscience
After the homily, the examination of conscience takes place;
a sample text is given in Appendix III, page 213. A period of
silence should always be included so that each person may
personally examine his conscience.

19. f) Act of repentance
After the examination of conscience, all say together:

I confess to almighty God,
and to you, my brothers and sisters,
that I have sinned through my own fault.
They strike their breast:
in my thoughts and in my words,
in what I have done,
and in what I have failed to do;
and I ask blessed Mary, ever virgin,
all the angels and saints,
and you, my brothers and sisters,
to pray for me to the Lord our God.

As a sign of conversion and charity toward others, it should
be suggested that the faithful give something to help the
poor to celebrate the feast of Easter with joy; or they might
visit the sick, or make up for some injustice in the community, or perform similar works.

Then the Lord's Prayer may be said, which the priest concludes in this way:

Deliver us, Father, from every evil
as we unite ourselves through penance
with the saving passion of your Son.
Grant us a share
in the joy of the resurrection of Jesus
who is Lord for ever and ever.
℞. **Amen.**

Depending on circumstances, the general confession may be
followed by a form of devotion such as adoration of the
cross or the way of the cross, according to local customs and
the wishes of the people.

At the end, an appropriate song is sung, and the people are
sent away with a greeting or blessing.

II. PENITENTIAL CELEBRATIONS DURING ADVENT

20. a) After an appropriate song and the greeting by the minister, the meaning of the celebration is explained in these or similar words:

My brothers and sisters, Advent is a time of preparation, when we make ready to celebrate the mystery of our Lord's coming as man, the beginning of our redemption. Advent also moves us to look forward with renewed hope to the second coming of Christ, when God's plan of salvation will be brought to fulfillment. We are reminded too of our Lord's coming to each one of us at the hour of our death. We must make sure that he will find us prepared for his coming, as the gospel tells us: "Blessed are those servants who are found awake when the Lord comes" Luke 12:37. **This service of penance is meant to make us ready in mind and heart for the coming of Christ, which we are soon to celebrate in the Mass of Christmas.**

Or:

Now it is time for you to wake from sleep, for our salvation is nearer to us than it was when we first believed. The night is ending; the day draws near. Let us then cast off the deeds of darkness and put on the armor of light. Let us live honestly as people do in the daylight, not in carousing and drunkenness, not in lust and debauchery, not in quarreling and jealousy. But rather let us put on the Lord Jesus Christ and give no thought to the desires of the flesh. Romans 13:11-12.

21. b) Prayer

My brothers and sisters, we look forward to celebrating the mystery of Christ's coming on the feast of Christmas. Let us pray that when he comes he may find us awake and ready to receive him.
All pray in silence for a brief period.

Lord our God,
maker of the heavens,
as we look forward to the coming of our redeemer
grant us the forgiveness of our sins.

We ask this through Christ our Lord.
℟. Amen.

Or:
Eternal Son of God,
creator of the human family
and our redeemer,
come at last among us
as the child of the immaculate Virgin,
and redeem the world.
Reveal your loving presence
by which you set us free from sin
in becoming one like us
in all things but sin,
for you live and reign for ever and ever.
℟. Amen.

22. c) Readings

First Reading
Malachi 3:1-7a
The Lord whom you seek will come to his temple.
A reading from the book of the prophet Malachi

Look, I am going to send my messenger
    to prepare a way before me.
And the Lord you are seeking will suddenly
    enter his Temple;
        and the angel of the covenant whom you are longing for,
        yes, he is coming, says the Lord of hosts.
Who will be able to resist
    the day of his coming?
Who will remain standing when he appears?
For he is like the refiner's fire and the fullers' alkali.
He will take his seat as refiner and purifier;
    he will purify the sons of Levi and refine them
        like gold and silver, and then they will make the offering
        to the Lord as it should be made.
The offering of Judah and Jerusalem will then be welcomed

by the Lord as in former days,
as in the years of old.
I mean to visit you for the judgment
and I am going to be a ready witness
against sorcerer, adulterer and perjurer,
against those who oppress the wage earner, the widow and the orphan,
and who rob the settler of his rights—
no need for you to be afraid of me, says the Lord of hosts.
No; I, the Lord, do not change;
and you, sons of Jacob, you are not ruined yet!
Since the days of your ancestors
you have evaded my statutes and not observed them.
Return to me and I will return to you,
says the Lord of hosts.
This is the Word of the Lord

Responsorial Psalm
Psalm 85:1-13
R̥. (8) **Lord, let us see your kindness, and grant us your salvation.**

O Lord, you once favored your land
and revived the fortunes of Jacob,
you forgave the guilt of your people
and covered all their sins.
You averted all your rage,
you calmed the heat of your anger.   R̥.

Revive us now, God our helper!
Put an end to your grievance against us.
Will you be angry with us for ever,
will your anger never cease?   R̥.

Will you not restore again our life
that your people may rejoice in you?
Let us see, O Lord, your mercy
and give us your saving help.   R̥.

I will hear what the Lord God has to say,
a voice that speaks of peace,
peace for his people and his friends
and those who turn to him in their hearts.
His help is near for those who fear him
and his glory will dwell in our land.   R̥.

Mercy and faithfulness have met;
justice and peace have embraced.

Faithfulness shall spring from the earth
and justice look down from heaven.
The Lord will make us prosper
and our earth shall yield its fruit. ℟.

Second Reading
Revelation 21:1-12
He will wipe away all the tears from their eyes.
A reading from the book of Revelation

Then I saw a new heaven and a new earth;
  the first heaven and the first earth had disappeared now,
  and there was no longer any sea.
I saw the holy city, and the new Jerusalem,
  coming down from God out of heaven,
  as beautiful as a bride all dressed for her husband.
Then I heard a loud voice call from the throne,
  "You see this city? Here God lives among men.
He will make his home among them;
  they shall be his people, and he will be their God;
  his name is God-with-them.
He will wipe away all tears from their eyes;
  there will be no more death,
  and no more mourning or sadness.
The world of the past has gone."
Then the One sitting on the throne spoke:
  "Now I am making the whole of creation new," he said.
"Write this: that what I am saying is sure
  and will come true."
And then he said, "It is already done.
I am the Alpha and the Omega, the Beginning and the End.
I will give water from the well of life
  free to anybody who is thirsty;
  it is the rightful inheritance
  of the one who proves victorious;
  and I will be his God and he a son to me.
But the legacy for cowards, for those who break their word,
  or worship obscenities, for murderers and fornicators,
  and for fortunetellers, idolaters or any other sort of liars,
  is the second death in the burning lake of sulphur."
One of the seven angels that had the seven bowls
  full of the seven last plagues came to speak to me,
  and said, "Come here and I will show you the bride
  that the Lamb has married."

In the spirit, he took me to the top
  of an enormous high mountain and showed me Jerusalem,
  the holy city, coming down from God out of heaven.
It had all the radiant glory of God
  and glittered like some precious jewel of crystal-clear diamond.
The walls of it were of a great height, and had twelve gates;
  at each of the twelve gates there was an angel,
  and over the gates were written the names
  of the twelve tribes of Israel.
This is the Word of the Lord.

Gospel
Verse before the gospel
I am coming quickly, says the Lord, and I will repay
    each man.
Come, Lord Jesus.

Or:

The Spirit and the Bride say: "Come."
Let all who hear answer: "Come."
Come, Lord Jesus.

Or another appropriate song may be sung.

Matthew 3:1-12
Repent, for the kingdom of heaven is close at hand.

✝ A reading from the holy gospel according to Matthew

In due course John the Baptist appeared;
  he preached in the wilderness of Judaea
  and this was his message:
  "Repent, for the kingdom of heaven is close at hand."
This was the man the prophet Isaiah spoke of
  when he said:

  A voice cries in the wilderness:
  prepare a way for the Lord,
  make his paths straight.

This man John wore a garment made of camel hair
  with a leather belt around his waist,
  and his food was locusts and wild honey.
Then Jerusalem and all Judaea
  and the whole Jordan district made their way to him,
  and as they were baptized by him in the river Jordan
  they confessed their sins.

But when he saw a number of Pharisees
and Sadducees coming for baptism he said to them,
"Brood of vipers,
who warned you to fly from the retribution that is coming?
But if you are repentant, produce the appropriate fruit,
and do not presume to tell yourselves,
'We have Abraham for our father,' because, I tell you,
God can raise children for Abraham from these stones.
Even now the ax is laid to the roots of the trees,
so that any tree which fails to produce good fruit
will be cut down and thrown on the fire.
I baptize you in water for repentance,
but the one who follows me is more powerful than I am,
and I am not fit to carry his sandals;
he will baptize you with the Holy Spirit and fire.
His winnowing fan is in his hand;
he will clear his threshing floor
and gather his wheat into the barn;
but the chaff he will burn in a fire that will never go out."
This is the gospel of the Lord.

Or:

Luke 3:3-17

All mankind shall see the salvation of God.

✝ A reading from the holy gospel according to Luke

John went through the whole Jordan district
proclaiming a baptism of repentance
for the forgiveness of sins,
as it is written in the book
of the sayings of the prophet Isaiah:

A voice cries in the wilderness:
Prepare a way for the Lord,
make his paths straight.
Every valley will be filled in,
every mountain and hill be laid low,
winding ways will be straightened
and rough roads made smooth.
And all mankind shall see the salvation of God.

He said, therefore,
to the crowds who came to be baptized by him,
"Brood of vipers,
who warned you to fly from the retribution that is coming?
But if you are repentant, produce the appropriate fruits,

and do not think of telling yourselves,
'We have Abraham for our father,' because, I tell you,
God can raise children for Abraham from these stones.
Yes, even now the ax is laid to the roots of the trees,
so that any tree which fails to produce good fruit
will be cut down and thrown on the fire."
When all the people asked him, "What must we do, then?"
he answered, "If anyone has two tunics
he must share with the man who has none,
and the one with something to eat must do the same."
There were tax collectors too who came for baptism,
and these said to him, "Master, what must we do?"
He said to them, "Exact no more than your rate."
Some soldiers asked him in their turn,
"What about us? What must we do?"
He said to them, "No intimidation! No extortion!
Be content with your pay!"
A feeling of expectancy had grown among the people,
who were beginning to think
that John might be the Christ,
so John declared before them all,
"I baptize you with water, but someone is coming,
someone who is more powerful than I am,
and I am not fit to undo the strap of his sandals;
he will baptize you with the Holy Spirit and fire.
His winnowing fan is in his hand
to clear his threshing floor
and to gather the wheat into his barn;
but the chaff he will burn in a fire that will never go out."
This is the gospel of the Lord.

23. d) Examination of conscience
After the homily, the examination of conscience takes place;
a sample text is given in Appendix III, page 213. A period of
silence should always be included so that each person may
personally examine his conscience.

24. e) Act of repentance
The act of repentance follows the examination of conscience.
All may say the **I confess to almighty God** or the inter-
cessions as in no. 60.

The Lord's Prayer is said or sung, and is concluded by the
presiding minister in this way:

Lord our God,
on the first day of creation
you made the light
that scatters all darkness.
Let Christ, the light of lights,
hidden from all eternity,
shine at last on your people
and free us from the darkness of sin.
Fill our lives with good works
as we go out to meet your Son,
so that we may give him a fitting welcome.

We ask this through Christ our Lord.
℟. Amen.

Or:
Almighty and eternal God,
you sent your only-begotten Son
to reconcile the world to yourself.
Lift from our hearts
the oppressive gloom of sin,
so that we may celebrate
the approaching dawn of Christ's birth
with fitting joy.

We ask this through Christ our Lord.
℟. Amen.

At the end, a song is sung, and the people are sent away
with a greeting or blessing.

III. COMMON PENITENTIAL CELEBRATIONS

I. SIN AND CONVERSION

25. a) After an appropriate song (for example Psalm
139:1-12, 16, 23-24) and greeting, the minister who presides
briefly explains the meaning of the readings. Then he invites
all to pray. After a period of silence, he concludes the prayer
in this way:

Lord Jesus,
you turned and looked on Peter
when he denied you for the third time.
He wept for his sin
and turned again to you in sincere repentance.
Look now on us and touch our hearts,
so that we also may turn back to you
and be always faithful in serving you,
for you live and reign for ever and ever.
R̸. Amen.

26. b) Readings

First Reading
Luke 22:31-34
I tell you, Peter: the cock will not crow today before you
deny me three times.
✝ A reading from the holy gospel according to Luke

"Simon, Simon! Satan, you must know,
   has got his wish to sift you all like wheat;
   but I have prayed for you, Simon,
   that your faith may not fail,
   and once you have recovered,
   you in your turn must strengthen your brothers."
"Lord," he answered,
   "I would be ready to go to prison with you, and to death."
Jesus replied, "I tell you, Peter,
   by the time the cock crows today
   you will have denied three times that you know me."
   This is the gospel of the Lord.

A short period of silence follows the reading.

Second Reading
Luke 22:54-62
Peter went out and wept bitterly.
✝ A reading from the holy gospel according to Luke

They seized Jesus then and led him away,
   and they took him to the high priest's house.
Peter followed at a distance.
They had lit a fire in the middle of the courtyard
   and Peter sat down among them,
   and as he was sitting there by the blaze

a servant girl saw him, peered at him, and said,
    "This person was with him too."
But he denied it.
"Woman," he said, "I do not know him."
Shortly afterward someone else saw him and said,
    "You are another of them."
But Peter replied, "I am not, my friend."
About an hour later another man insisted, saying,
    "This fellow was certainly with him.
Why, he is a Galilean."
"My friend," said Peter,
    "I do not know what you are talking about."
At that instant, while he was still speaking, the cock crew,
    and the Lord turned and looked straight at Peter,
    and Peter remembered what the Lord had said to him,
    "Before the cock crows today,
    you will have disowned me three times."
And he went outside and wept bitterly.
This is the gospel of the Lord.

Responsorial Psalm
Psalm 3 1:10, 15-17, 20 or Psalm 51 (page 86) or another
appropriate song.

R̷. My trust is in you, O Lord.

He frustrates the designs of the nations,
he defeats the plans of the peoples.   R̷.

From the place where he dwells he gazes
on all the dwellers on the earth,
he who shapes the hearts of them all
and considers all their deeds.   R̷.

Our soul is waiting for the Lord.
The Lord is our help and our shield.   R̷.

Gospel
John 21:15-19
Simon, son of John, do you love me?

✝ A reading from the holy gospel according to John

After the meal Jesus said to Simon Peter,
    "Simon son of John,
    do you love me more than these others do?"
He answered, "Yes Lord, you know I love you."
Jesus said to him, "Feed my lambs."
A second time he said to him,

"Simon son of John, do you love me?"
He replied, "Yes, Lord, you know I love you."
Jesus said to him, "Look after my sheep."
Then he said to him a third time,
"Simon son of John, do you love me?"
Peter was upset that he asked him the third time,
   "Do you love me?" and said,
"Lord, you know everything; you know I love you."
Jesus said to him, "Feed my sheep.

"I tell you most solemnly,
when you were young
you put on your own belt
and walked where you like;
but when you grow old
you will stretch out your hands,
and somebody else will put a belt around you
and take you where you would rather not go.

In these words he indicated the kind of death
   by which Peter would give glory to God.
After this he said, "Follow me."
This is the gospel of the Lord.

27. c) Homily
The celebrant may speak about:
—the trust we must put in God's grace, not in our own powers;
—the faithfulness by which we as baptized Christians must live as true and faithful followers of the Lord;
—our weakness by which we often fall into sin and refuse to give witness to the gospel;
—the mercy of the Lord, who welcomes as a friend the one who turns to him with his whole heart.

28. d) Examination of conscience
After the homily, the examination of conscience takes place; a sample text is given in Appendix III, page 213. A period of silence should always be included so that each person may personally examine his conscience.

29. e) Act of repentance
After the examination of conscience, the presiding minister invites all to prayer in these or similar words:

God gives us an example of love: when we were
sinners he first loved us and took pity on us. Let us
turn to him with a sincere heart, and in the words of
Peter say to him:
℟. Lord, you know all things; you know that I love
you.

A short period of silence should follow each invocation.
Each invocation may be said by different individuals, the
rest answering.

—Lord, like Peter we have relied on our own strength
rather than on grace. Look on us, Lord, and have
mercy.
℟. Lord, you know all things; you know that I love
you.

—Our pride and foolishness have led us into temptation. Look on us, Lord, and have mercy.
℟. Lord, you know all things; you know that I love
you.

—We have been vain and self-important. Look on us,
Lord, and have mercy.
℟. Lord, you know all things; you know that I love
you.

—We have at times been pleased rather than sad-
dened by the misfortunes of others. Look on us, Lord,
and have mercy.
℟. Lord, you know all things; you know that I love
you.

—We have shown indifference for those in need instead of helping them. Look on us, Lord, and have
mercy.
℟. Lord, you know all things; you know that I love
you.

—We have been afraid to stand up for justice and
truth. Look on us, Lord, and have mercy.
℟. Lord, you know all things; you know that I love
you.

—We have repeatedly broken the promises of our
baptism and failed to be your disciples. Look on us,
Lord, and have mercy.
R̷. Lord, you know all things; you know that I love
you.

—Let us now pray to the Father in the words Christ
gave us and ask forgiveness for our sins:
Our Father . . .

30. f) After an appropriate song, the presiding minister says
the final prayer and dismisses the people:

Lord Jesus, our Savior,
you called Peter to be an apostle;
when he repented of his sin
you restored him to your friendship
and confirmed him as first of the apostles.
Turn to us with love
and help us to imitate Peter's example.
Give us strength to turn from our sins
and to serve you in the future
with greater love and devotion,
for you live and reign for ever and ever.
R̷. Amen.

II. THE SON RETURNS TO THE FATHER

31. a) After an appropriate song and the greeting by the
minister, the theme of the celebration is explained to the
community. Then he invites all to pray. After a period of
silence, he says:

Almighty God,
you are the Father of us all.
You created the human family
to dwell for ever with you
and to praise your glory.
Open our ears to hear your voice
so that we may return to you
with sincere repentance for our sins.

Teach us to see in you our loving Father,
full of compassion for all who call to you for help.
We know that you punish us only to set us free from
  evil
and that you are ready to forgive us our sins.
Restore your gift of salvation
which alone brings true happiness,
so that we may all return to our Father's house
and share your table
now and for ever.
℟. Amen.

32. b) Readings

First Reading
Ephesians 1:3-7
He chose us from all eternity to be his adopted sons and
daughters.

A reading from the letter of Paul to the Ephesians

Blessed be God the Father of our Lord Jesus Christ,
who has blessed us with all the spiritual blessings of heaven in
  Christ.
Before the world was made, he chose us, chose us in Christ,
to be holy and spotless, and to live through love in his presence,
determining that we should become his adopted sons, through
  Jesus Christ
for his own kind purposes,
to make us praise the glory of his grace,
his free gift to us in the Beloved,
in whom, through his blood, we gain our freedom, the
  forgiveness of our sins.
  This is the Word of the Lord.

Responsorial Psalm
Psalm 27:1, 4, 7-10, 13-14
℟. **The Lord is my light and my help.**

The Lord is my light and my help;
whom shall I fear?
The Lord is the stronghold of my life;
before whom shall I shrink?   ℟.

There is one thing I ask of the Lord,
for this I long,
to live in the house of the Lord,

all the days of my life,
to savor the sweetness of the Lord,
to behold his temple. R⁊.

O Lord, hear my voice when I call;
have mercy and answer.
Of you my heart has spoken:
'Seek his face.' R⁊.

It is your face, O Lord, that I seek;
hide not your face.
Dismiss not your servant in anger;
you have been my help. R⁊.

Do not abandon or forsake me,
O God my help!
Though father and mother forsake me,
The Lord will receive me. R⁊.

I am sure I shall see the Lord's goodness
in the land of the living.
Hope in him, hold firm and take heart.
Hope in the Lord! R⁊.

Gospel
Luke 15:11-32
His father saw him and was filled with pity.
(See above, page 166)

33. c) Homily
The minister may speak about:
—sin as a turning away from the love that we should have
for God our Father;
—the limitless mercy of our Father for his children who
have sinned;
—the nature of true conversion;
—the forgiveness we should extend to our brothers;
—the eucharistic banquet as the culmination of our reconciliation with the Church and with God.

34. d) Examination of conscience
After the homily, the examination of conscience takes place;
a sample text is given in Appendix III, page 213. A period of
silence should always be included so that each person may
personally examine his conscience.

35. e) Act of repentance
After the examination of conscience, the presiding minister
invites all to pray:

**Our God is a God of mercy, slow to anger and full of
patience. He is the father who welcomes his son when
he returns from a distant country. Let us pray to him
with trust in his goodness:**
R̷. We are not worthy to be called your children.

**—By our misuse of your gifts we have sinned against
you.**
R̷. We are not worthy to be called your children.

**—By straying from you in mind and heart we have
sinned against you.**
R̷. We are not worthy to be called your children.

—By forgetting your love we have sinned against you.
R̷. We are not worthy to be called your children.

**—By indulging ourselves, while neglecting our true
good and the good of our neighbor, we have sinned
against you.**
R̷. We are not worthy to be called your children.

**—By failing to help our neighbor in his need we have
sinned against you.**
R̷. We are not worthy to be called your children.

**—By being slow to forgive we have sinned against
you.**
R̷. We are not worthy to be called your children.

**—By failing to remember your repeated forgiveness
we have sinned against you.**
R̷. We are not worthy to be called your children.

Members of the congregation may add other invocations. A
brief period of silence should follow each invocation. It may
be desirable to have different individuals say each invocation.

**—Let us now call upon our Father in the words that
Jesus gave us, and ask him to forgive us our sins:
Our Father . . .**

36. f) After an appropriate song, the presiding minister says
the final prayer and dismisses the people:

**God our Father,
you chose us to be your children,
to be holy in your sight
and happy in your presence.
Receive us as a loving Father
so that we may share the joy and love
of your holy Church.**

**We ask this through Christ our Lord.
℞. Amen.**

III. THE BEATITUDES

37. a) After an appropriate song and greeting of the
minister, the person presiding explains briefly the meaning
of the readings. Then he invites all to pray. After a period of
silence, he says:

**Lord,
open our ears and our hearts today
to the message of your Son,
so that through the power of his death and
    resurrection
we may walk in newness of life.**

**We ask this through Christ our Lord.
℞. Amen.**

38. b) Readings

First Reading
1 John 1:5-9
If we say that we have no sin, we are deceiving ourselves.
A reading from the first letter of John

**This is what we have heard from him,
and the message that we are announcing to you:
God is light; there is no darkness in him at all.
If we say that we are in union with God
while we are living in darkness,
we are lying because we are not living the truth.
But if we live our lives in the light,**

as he is in the light,
we are in union with one another,
and the blood of Jesus, his Son,
purifies us from all sin.

If we say we have no sin in us,
we are deceiving ourselves
and refusing to admit the truth;
but if we acknowledge our sins,
then God who is faithful and just
will forgive our sins and purify us
from everything that is wrong.
This is the Word of the Lord.

Responsorial Psalm (See Isaiah 35:4)
Psalm 146:5-10
R̷. Lord, come and save us.

Our Lord is great and almighty;
his wisdom can never be measured.
The Lord raises the lowly;
he humbles the wicked to the dust.
O sing to the Lord, giving thanks;
sing psalms to our God with the harp.   R̷.

He covers the heavens with clouds;
he prepares the rain for the earth,
making mountains sprout with grass
and with plants to serve man's needs.   R̷.

He provides the beasts with their food
and young ravens that call upon him.   R̷.

His delight is not in horses
nor his pleasure in warriors' strength.   R̷.

Gospel
Matthew 5:1-10
Happy are the poor in spirit, for theirs is the kingdom of
heaven.
✠ A reading from the holy gospel according to Matthew
Seeing the crowds, he went up the hill.
There he sat down and was joined by his disciples.
Then he began to speak.
This is what he taught them:

"How happy are the poor in spirit;
theirs is the kingdom of heaven.
Happy the gentle:
they shall have the earth for their heritage.
Happy those who mourn:
they shall be comforted.
Happy those who hunger and thirst for what is right:
they shall be satisfied.
Happy the merciful:
they shall have mercy shown them.
Happy the pure in heart:
they shall see God.
Happy the peacemakers:
they shall be called sons of God.
Happy those who are persecuted in the cause of right:
theirs is the kingdom of heaven.

This is the gospel of the Lord.

39. c) Homily
The minister may speak about:
—sin, by which we ignore the commandments of Christ and
act contrary to the teaching of the beatitudes;
—the firmness of our faith in the words of Jesus;
—our faithfulness in imitating Christ in our private lives, in
the Christian community, and in human society;
—each beatitude.

40. d) Examination of conscience
After the homily, the examination of conscience takes place;
a sample text is given in Appendix III, page 213. A period of
silence should always be included so that each person may
personally examine his conscience.

41. e) Act of repentance
After the examination of conscience, the presiding minister
invites all to pray in these or similar words:

**My brothers and sisters, Jesus Christ has left an
example for us to follow. Humbly and confidently let
us ask him to renew us in spirit so that we may shape
our lives according to the teaching of his Gospel.**

—Lord Jesus Christ, you said:
"Blessed are the poor in spirit,
for theirs is the kingdom of heaven."
Yet we are preoccupied with money and worldly
goods
and even try to increase them at the expense of
justice.
Lamb of God, you take away the sin of the world:
R⁷. Have mercy on us.

—Lord Jesus Christ, you said:
"Blessed are the gentle,
for they shall inherit the earth."
Yet we are ruthless with each other,
and our world is full of discord and violence.
Lamb of God, you take away the sin of the world:
R⁷. Have mercy on us.

—Lord Jesus Christ, you said:
"Blessed are those who mourn,
for they shall be comforted."
Yet we are impatient under our own burdens
and unconcerned about the burdens of others.
Lamb of God, you take away the sin of the world:
R⁷. Have mercy on us.

—Lord Jesus Christ, you said:
"Blessed are those who hunger and thirst for justice,
for they shall be filled."
Yet we do not thirst for you, the fountain of all
holiness,
and are slow to spread your influence
in our private lives or in society.
Lamb of God, you take away the sin of the world:
R⁷. Have mercy on us.

—Lord Jesus Christ, you said:
"Blessed are the merciful,
for they shall receive mercy."
Yet we are slow to forgive
and quick to condemn.
Lamb of God, you take away the sin of the world:
R⁷. Have mercy on us.

—Lord Jesus Christ, you said:
"Blessed are the clean of heart,
for they shall see God."
Yet we are prisoners of our senses and evil desires
and dare not raise our eyes to you.
Lamb of God, you take away the sin of the world:
R̝. Have mercy on us.

—Lord Jesus Christ, you said:
"Blessed are the peacemakers,
for they shall be called children of God."
Yet we fail to make peace in our families,
in our country, and in the world.
Lamb of God, you take away the sin of the world:
R̝. Have mercy on us.

—Lord Jesus Christ, you said:
"Blessed are those who are persecuted
for the sake of justice,
for the kingdom of heaven is theirs."
Yet we prefer to practice injustice
rather than suffer for the sake of right;
we discriminate against our neighbors
and oppress and persecute them.
Lamb of God, you take away the sin of the world:
R̝. Have mercy on us.

—Now let us turn to God our Father and ask him to
free us from evil and prepare us for the coming of his
kingdom:
Our Father . . .

42. f) After an appropriate song, the presiding minister says
the final prayer and dismisses the people:

Lord Jesus Christ,
gentle and humble of heart,
full of compassion and maker of peace,
you lived in poverty
and were persecuted in the cause of justice.
You chose the cross as the path to glory
to show us the way to salvation.
May we receive with joyful hearts

the word of your Gospel
and live by your example
as heirs and citizens of your kingdom,
where you live and reign for ever and ever.
℟. **Amen.**

IV. FOR CHILDREN

43. This service is suitable for younger children, including those who have not yet participated in the sacrament of penance.

Theme:

GOD COMES TO LOOK FOR US

44. The penitential celebration should be prepared with the children so that they will understand its meaning and purpose, be familiar with the songs, have at least an elementary knowledge of the biblical text to be read, and know what they are to say and in what order.

45. a)   Greeting
When the children have come together in the church or some other suitable place, the celebrant greets them in a friendly manner. Briefly he reminds them why they have come together and recounts the theme of the service. After the greeting, an opening song may be sung.

46. b)   Reading
The celebrant may give a short introduction to the reading in these or similar words:

My dear children, each one of us has been baptized,
and so we are all sons and daughters of God. God
loves us as a Father, and he asks us to love him with
all our hearts. He also wants us to be good to each
other, so that we may all live happily together.

But people do not always do what God wants. They
say: "I will not obey! I am going to do as I please."
They disobey God and do not want to listen to him.
We, too, often act like that.

That is what we call sin. When we sin we turn our backs on God. If we do something really bad we cut ourselves off from God; we are complete strangers to him.

What does God do when someone turns away from him? What does he do when we leave the path of goodness that he has shown us, when we run the risk of losing the life of grace he has given us? Does God turn away from us when we turn away from him by our sins?

Here is what God does, in the words of Jesus himself:

47. Only one text of Scripture should be read.

Luke 15:1-7
Heaven is filled with joy when one sinner turns back to God.

✝ A reading from the holy gospel according to Luke

The tax collectors and the sinners, meanwhile,
   were all seeking his company to hear what he had to say,
   and the Pharisees and the scribes complained.
"This man," they said,
   "welcomes sinners and eats with them."
So he spoke this parable to them:

"What man among you with a hundred sheep,
   losing one,
   would not leave the ninety-nine in the wilderness
   and go after the missing one till he found it?
And when he found it,
   would he not joyfully take it on his shoulders and then,
   when he got home,
   call together his friends and neighbors?
'Rejoice with me,' he would say,
   'I have found my sheep that was lost.'
In the same way, I tell you,
   there will be more rejoicing in heaven
   over one repentant sinner
   than over ninety-nine virtuous men
   who have no need of repentance.
This is the gospel of the Lord.

48. c)   Homily
The homily should be short, proclaiming God's love for us
and preparing the ground for the examination of conscience.

49. d)   Examination of conscience
The celebrant should adapt the examination to the children's
level of understanding by brief comments. There should be
a suitable period of silence (see Appendix III, page 213).

50. e)   Act of repentance
This litany may be said by the celebrant or by one or more of
the children, alternating with all present. Before the response, which may be sung, all should observe a brief
pause.

God our Father,

——**Sometimes we have not behaved as your children
should.**
R̠. **But you love us and come to us.**

——**We have given trouble to our parents and
teachers.**
R̠. **But you love us and come to us.**

——**We have quarrelled and called each other names.**
R̠. **But you love us and come to us.**

——**We have been lazy at home and in school, and
have not been helpful to our parents (brothers, sisters,
friends).**
R̠. **But you love us and come to us.**

——**We have thought too much of ourselves and have
told lies.**
R̠. **But you love us and come to us.**

——**We have not done good to others when we had
the chance.**
R̠. **But you love us and come to us.**

**Now with Jesus, our brother, we come before our
Father in heaven and ask him to forgive our sins:
Our Father . . .**

51. f) Act of contrition and purpose of amendment
Sorrow may be shown by some sign, for example, individual
children may come to the altar or another suitable place with
a candle, and light it there; if necessary, a server may help.
Each child says in his own words:

Father,
I am sorry for all my sins:
for what I have done
and for what I have failed to do.
I will sincerely try to do better
especially . . .
(he mentions his particular resolution).
Help me to walk by your light.

In place of the candle, or in addition to it, the children may
prepare a written prayer or resolution and place it on the
altar or on a table designated for this purpose.

If the number of children or other circumstances do not
allow for this, the celebrant asks the children present to say
the above prayer together, along with a general resolution.

52. g) Prayer of the celebrant

God our Father always seeks us out
when we walk away from the path of goodness.
He is always ready to forgive
when we have sinned.
May almighty God have mercy on us,
forgive us our sins,
and bring us to everlasting life.
R̠. Amen.

53. The minister invites the children to express their thanks
to God. They may do this by an appropriate hymn.

Then he dismisses them.

V. FOR YOUNG PEOPLE

54. The penitential celebration should be prepared with the
young people so that with the celebrant, they may choose or

compose the texts and songs. The readers, cantors or choir should be chosen from among them.

Theme:

RENEWAL OF OUR LIVES ACCORDING TO THE CHRISTIAN VOCATION

55. a) Greeting
This may be given in these or similar words:

Dear friends, we have come here to do penance and to make a fresh start as Christians. Many people see in penance only its difficult side, and its emphasis on sorrow. But it has also a more joyful side, and it looks more to the future than to the past.

Through penance God calls us to a new beginning. He helps us to find our true freedom as his sons and daughters. When Jesus invites us to repentance, he is inviting us to take our place in his Father's kingdom. This is what he teaches us in the parable about the merchant who came across a pearl of great value and sold everything he had in order to buy it.

If we follow our Lord's advice we exchange our past life for one far more valuable.

Then a song is sung; it should stress the call to a new life or following God's call with an eager heart (for example, Psalm 41:1-9, 41).

℟. **Here am I, Lord; I come to do your will.**

**Like the deer that yearns
for running streams,
so my soul is yearning
for you, my God.**

**My soul is thirsting for God,
the God of my life;
when can I enter and see
the face of God?**

**My tears have become my bread,
by night, by day,
as I hear it said all the day long:
'Where is your God?'**

These things will I remember
as I pour out my soul:
how I would lead the rejoicing crowd
into the house of God,
amid cries of gladness and thanksgiving,
the throng wild with joy.

Why are you cast down, my soul,
why groan within me?
Hope in God; I will praise him still,
my savior and my God.

My soul is cast down within me
as I think of you,
from the country of Jordan and Mount Hermon,
from the Hill of Mizar.

Deep is calling on deep,
in the roar of waters:
your torrents and all your waves
swept over me.

By day the Lord will send
his loving kindness;
by night I will sing to him,
praise the God of my life.

56. b) Prayer

Lord our God,
you call us out of darkness into light,
out of self-deception into truth,
out of death into life.
Send us your Holy Spirit
to open our ears to your call.
Fill our hearts with courage
to be true followers of your Son.
We ask this through Christ our Lord.
R̷. Amen.

57. c) Readings

First Reading
Romans 7:18-25
Unhappy man am I! Who will free me? Thanks to God
through Jesus Christ our Lord.

A reading from the letter of Paul to the Romans
The fact is, I know of nothing good living in me—
  living, that is, in my unspiritual self—
  for though the will to do what is good is in me,
  the performance is not,
  with the result that instead of doing the good things
  I want to do,
  I carry out the sinful things I do not want.
When I act against my will, then,
  it is not my true self doing it, but sin which lives in me.
In fact, this seems to be the rule,
  that every single time I want to do good
  it is something evil that comes to hand.
In my inmost self I dearly love God's Law,
  but I can see that my body follows a different law
  that battles against the law which my reason dictates.
This is what makes me a prisoner of that law of sin
  which lives inside my body.
What a wretched man I am!
Who will rescue me from this body doomed to death?
Thanks be to God through Jesus Christ our Lord!
In short,
  it is I who with my reason serve the Law of God,
  and no less I
  who serve in my unspiritual self the law of sin.

This is the Word of the Lord.

or:
Romans 8:19-23
We know that by turning everything to their good, God
cooperates with all those who love him.

A reading from the letter of Paul to the Romans

The whole creation
  is eagerly waiting for God to reveal his sons.
It was not for any fault on the part of creation
  that it was made unable to attains its purpose,
  it was made so by God;
  but creation still retains the hope of being freed,
  like us, from its slavery to decadence,
  to enjoy the same freedom and glory as the children of God.
From the beginning till now the entire creation,
  as we know,
  has been groaning in one great act of giving birth;

and not only creation,
but all of us who possess the first fruits of the Spirit,
we too groan inwardly
as we wait for our bodies to be set free.
This is the Word of the Lord.

A song is sung, or a brief period of silence is observed.

Gospel
Matthew 13:44-46
He sold all that he had and bought the field.

✝ A reading from the gospel according to Matthew

"The kingdom of heaven is like treasure
  hidden in a field which someone has found;
  he hides it again, goes off happy,
  sells everything he owns and buys the field.
"Again, the kingdom of heaven is like a merchant
  looking for fine pearls;
  when he finds one of great value
  he goes and sells everything he owns and buys it.
This is the gospel of the Lord.

58. d) Homily
The celebrant may speak about:
——the law of sin which in us struggles against God;
——the necessity of giving up the way of sin so that we may
enter the kingdom of God.

59. e) Examination of conscience
After the homily, the examination of conscience takes place;
a sample text is given in Appendix III, page 213. A period of
silence should always be included so that each person may
personally examine his conscience.

60. f) Act of repentance
Christ our Lord came to call sinners into his Father's
kingdom. Let us now make an act of sorrow in our
hearts and resolve to avoid sin in the future.

After a brief period of silence, all say together:
I confess to almighty God,
and to you, my brothers and sisters,
that I have sinned through my own fault
They strike their breast:

in my thoughts and in my words,
in what I have done,
and in what I have failed to do;
and I ask blessed Mary, ever virgin,
all the angels and saints,
and you, my brothers and sisters,
to pray for me to the Lord our God.

Minister:
Lord our God,
you know all things.
You know that we want to be more generous
in serving you and our neighbor.
Look on us with love and hear our prayer.

Reader:
Give us the strength to turn away from sin.
R̷. Hear our prayer.

Help us to be sorry for our sins and to keep our
resolutions.
R̷. Hear our prayer.

Forgive our sins and have pity on our weakness.
R̷. Hear our prayer.

Give us trust in your goodness and make us generous
in serving you.
R̷. Hear our prayer.

Help us to be true followers of your Son and living
members of his Church.

Minister:
God does not want the sinner to die, but to turn to
him and live. May he be pleased that we have
confessed our sinfulness, and may he show us his
mercy as we pray in obedience to his Son.

All say together:
Our Father . . .

61. The celebration ends with an appropriate song and the
dismissal.

VI. FOR THE SICK

62. According to the condition of the sick people and the suitability of the place, the minister goes to the sick, gathered in one room, or else he brings them together in the sanctuary or church. He should adapt carefully the texts and their number to the condition of those who take part in the service. Since in most instances none of the sick will be able to act as reader, the minister should, if possible, invite another person to carry out this office.

Theme:

THE TIME OF SICKNESS IS A TIME OF GRACE

63. a) Greeting
He may greet them in these or similar words:

My dear friends, when Jesus came to preach repentance, he was bringing us good news, for he was proclaiming to us God's love and mercy. Again and again God comes to our help so that we may turn to him and live our lives entirely in his service. Penance is his gift, a gift we should accept with gratitude. Keeping this in mind, let us open our hearts to God with great simplicity and humility and ask to be reconciled with him as we now forgive each other.

If possible, a penitential song is sung by the sick persons, or by a choir.

64. b) Prayer
**Lord our God,
source of all goodness and mercy,
we come together as your family
to ask your forgiveness
and the forgiveness of each other.
Give us true sorrow for our sins
and loving trust in your compassion
so that we may acknowledge our sins
with sincere hearts.
Through this celebration
restore us to fuller union with yourself**

and with our neighbor
so that we may serve you with greater generosity.

We ask this through Christ our Lord.
℟. **Amen.**

65. c) Readings
The readings may be introduced in these or similar words:

**Many people enjoy good health and other blessings
and accept them as a matter of course, with no sense
of gratitude. In time of sickness we discover that all
these are great gifts, and that without them we easily
lose heart. God allows us to experience sickness in
order to test our faith. What is more, if we see our
suffering as a share in Christ's suffering, it can be of
great value both to ourselves and to the Church. The
time of sickness is not then wasted or meaningless. It
is in fact a time of grace if we accept it as God wants
us to accept it. This celebration is meant to help us to
do so. We shall therefore listen to God's word,
examine our conscience, and pray with sincere hearts.**

66. First Reading
James 5:13-16
The prayer of faith will save the sick man.

A reading from the letter of James

**If any one of you is in trouble, he should pray;
  if anyone is feeling happy, he should sing a psalm.
If one of you is ill,
  he should send for the elders of the church,
  and they must anoint him with oil in the name of the Lord
  and pray over him.
The prayer of faith will save the sick man
  and the Lord will raise him up again;
  and if he has committed any sins, he will be forgiven.
This is the Word of the Lord.**

Responsorial Psalm
Between the readings, a psalm may be said or sung
alternately, for example, Psalm 130 or Psalm 51.

Gospel
Mark 2:1-12
The Son of Man has authority on earth to forgive sins.
☩ A reading from the holy gospel according to Mark

When he returned to Capernaum some time later,
  word went around that he was back;
  and so many people collected that there was no room left,
  even in front of the door.
He was preaching the word to them when some people came
  bringing him a paralytic carried by four men,
  but as the crowd made it impossible to get the man to him,
  they stripped the roof over the place where Jesus was;
  and when they had made an opening,
  they lowered the stretcher on which the paralytic lay.
Seeing their faith, Jesus said to the paralytic,
  "My child, your sins are forgiven."
Now some scribes were sitting there,
  and they thought to themselves,
"How can this man talk like that? He is blaspheming.
Who can forgive sins but God?"
Jesus, inwardly aware that this was what they were thinking,
  said to them,
  "Why do you have these thoughts in your hearts?
  Which of these is easier:
  to say to the paralytic, 'Your sins are forgiven'
  or to say, 'Get up, pick up your stretcher and walk?'
But to prove to you that the Son of Man
  has authority on earth to forgive sins,"—
  he said to the paralytic—
  "I order you: get up, pick up your stretcher, and go off home."
And the man got up, picked up his stretcher at once
  and walked out in front of everyone,
  so that they were all astounded and praised God saying,
  "We have never seen anything like this."
  This is the gospel of the Lord.

67. d) Homily
It is fitting that the celebrant speak of sickness, dwelling not
so much on sickness of the body as on sickness of the soul.
He should emphasize the power of Jesus and his Church to
forgive sins and the value of suffering offered for others.

68. e) Examination of conscience

After the homily, the examination of conscience takes place; a sample text is given in Appendix III, page 213. A period of silence should always be included so that each person may personally examine his conscience.

The following questions may be added but adapted to the condition of the sick:

——Do I trust God's goodness and providence, even in times of stress and illness?

——Do I give in to sickness, to despair, to other unworthy thoughts and feelings?

——Do I fill my empty moments with reflection on life and with prayer to God?

——Do I accept my illness and pain as an opportunity for suffering with Christ, who redeemed us by his passion?

——Do I live by faith, confident that patience in suffering is of great benefit to the Church?

——Am I thoughtful of others and attentive to my fellow patients and their needs?

——Am I grateful to those who look after me and visit me?

——Do I give a good Christian example to others?

——Am I sorry for my past sins, and do I try to make amends for them by my patient acceptance of weakness and illness.

69. f) Act of repentance

After a moment of silence, all say together:

I confess to almighty God,
and to you, my brothers and sisters,
that I have sinned through my own fault

They strike their breast:

in my thoughts and in my words,
in what I have done,
and in what I have failed to do;
and I ask blessed Mary, ever virgin,
all the angels and saints,

and you, my brothers and sisters,
to pray for me to the Lord our God.

Reader:
Lord our God, we bear the name of your Son and call
you Father. We are sorry for our sins against you and
against our brothers and sisters.
R̸. Give us true repentance and sincere love for you
and for our neighbor.

Lord Jesus Christ, you redeemed us by your passion
and cross and gave us an example of patience and
love. We are sorry for our sins against you, and
especially for failing to serve you and our brothers
and sisters.
R̸. Give us true repentance and sincere love for you
and for our neighbor.

Holy Spirit, Lord, you speak to us in the Church and
in our conscience and inspire within us the desire to
do good. We are sorry for our sins against you, and
especially for our obstinate refusal to obey you.
R̸. Give us true repentance and sincere love for you
and for our neighbor.

Minister:
Let us ask God our Father to forgive us and to free us
from evil:
Our Father . . .

70. Then, if possible, the choir or the assembled people sing
a song, and the service concludes with a prayer of
thanksgiving:

71.
God of consolation and Father of mercies,
you forgive the sinner who acknowledges his guilt:
R̸. We praise you and thank you.

God of consolation and Father of mercies,
you give to those who suffer hardship or pain
a share in the sufferings of your Son

for the salvation of the world:
R̷. We praise you and thank you.

God of consolation and Father of mercies,
you look with love on those who are troubled or in
    sorrow;
you give them hope of salvation
and the promise of eternal life:
R̷. We praise you and thank you.

Let us pray.
Lord,
your goodness and mercy are boundless.
Look on your sons and daughters
gathered here in the name of your Son.
We thank you for all your gifts
and ask you to keep us always as your family,
full of living faith, firm hope,
and sincere love for you and for our neighbor.
We ask this through Christ our Lord.
R̷. Amen.

72. In place of the prayer, the service may end with a
blessing.

May the God of peace
fill your hearts with every blessing.
May he sustain you
with his gifts of hope and consolation,
help you to offer your lives in his service,
and bring you safely to eternal glory.
May almighty God,
the Father, and the Son, ✚ and the Holy Spirit,
grant you all that is good.
R̷. Amen.

73. The minister dismisses the assembly, or invites those
present to a friendly visit with the sick.

APPENDIX III

FORM OF EXAMINATION OF CONSCIENCE

1. This suggested form for an examination of conscience should be completed and adapted to meet the needs of different individuals and to follow local usages.

2. In an examination of conscience, before the sacrament of penance, each individual should ask himself these questions in particular:

1. **What is my attitude to the sacrament of penance? Do I sincerely want to be set free from sin, to turn again to God, to begin a new life, and to enter into a deeper friendship with God? Or do I look on it as a burden, to be undertaken as seldom as possible?**

2. **Did I forget to mention, or deliberately conceal, any grave sins in past confessions?**

3. **Did I perform the penance I was given? Did I make reparation for any injury to others? Have I tried to put into practice my resolution to lead a better life in keeping with the Gospel?**

3. Each individual should examine his life in the light of God's word.

I. The Lord says: "You shall love the Lord your God with your whole heart."

1. **Is my heart set on God, so that I really love him above all things and am faithful to his commandments, as a son loves his father? Or am I more concerned about the things of this world? Have I a right intention in what I do?**

2. **God spoke to us in his Son. Is my faith in God firm and secure? Am I wholehearted in accepting the Church's teaching? Have I been careful to grow in my understanding of the faith, to hear God's word, to**

listen to instructions on the faith, to avoid dangers to faith? Have I been always strong and fearless in professing my faith in God and the Church? Have I been willing to be known as a Christian in private and public life?

3. Have I prayed morning and evening? When I pray, do I really raise my mind and heart to God or is it a matter of words only? Do I offer God my difficulties, my joys, and my sorrows? Do I turn to God in time of temptation?

4. Have I love and reverence for God's name? Have I offended him in blasphemy, swearing falsely, or taking his name in vain? Have I shown disrespect for the Blessed Virgin Mary and the saints?

5. Do I keep Sundays and feast days holy by taking a full part, with attention and devotion, in the liturgy, and especially in the Mass? Have I fulfilled the precept of annual confession and of communion during the Easter season?

6. Are there false gods that I worship by giving them greater attention and deeper trust than I give to God: money, superstition, spiritism, or other occult practices?

II. The Lord says: "Love one another as I have loved you."

1. Have I a genuine love for my neighbors? Or do I use them for my own ends, or do to them what I would not want done to myself? Have I given grave scandal by my words or actions?

2. In my family life, have I contributed to the well-being and happiness of the rest of the family by patience and genuine love? Have I been obedient to parents, showing them proper respect and giving them help in their spiritual and material needs? Have I been careful to give a Christian upbringing to my children, and to help them by good example and by

exercising authority as a parent? Have I been faithful to my husband (wife) in my heart and in my relations with others?

3. Do I share my possessions with the less fortunate? Do I do my best to help the victims of oppression, misfortune, and poverty? Or do I look down on my neighbor, especially the poor, the sick, the elderly, strangers, and people of other races?

4. Does my life reflect the mission I received in confirmation? Do I share in the apostolic and charitable works of the Church and in the life of my parish? Have I helped to meet the needs of the Church and of the world and prayed for them: for the unity in the Church, for the spread of the Gospel among the nations, for peace and justice, etc.?

5. Am I concerned for the good and prosperity of the human community in which I live, or do I spend my life caring only for myself? Do I share to the best of my ability in the work of promoting justice, morality, harmony, and love in human relations? Have I done my duty as a citizen? Have I paid my taxes?

6. In my work or profession am I just, hard-working, honest, serving society out of love for others? Have I paid a fair wage to my employees? Have I been faithful to my promises and contracts?

7. Have I obeyed legitimate authority and given it due respect?

8. If I am in a position of responsibility or authority, do I use this for my own advantage or for the good of others, in a spirit of service?

9. Have I been truthful and fair, or have I injured others by deceit, calumny, detraction, rash judgment, or violation of a secret?

10. Have I done violence to others by damage to life or limb, reputation, honor, or material possessions? Have I involved them in loss? Have I been responsi-

ble for advising an abortion or procuring one? Have I kept up hatred for others? Am I estranged from others through quarrels, enmity, insults, anger? Have I been guilty of refusing to testify to the innocence of another because of selfishness?

11. Have I stolen the property of others? Have I desired it unjustly and inordinately? Have I damaged it? Have I made restitution of other people's property and made good their loss?

12. If I have been injured, have I been ready to make peace for the love of Christ and to forgive, or do I harbor hatred and the desire for revenge?

III. Christ our Lord says: "Be perfect as your Father is perfect."

1. Where is my life really leading me? Is the hope of eternal life my inspiration? Have I tried to grow in the life of the Spirit through prayer, reading the word of God and meditating on it, receiving the sacraments, self-denial? Have I been anxious to control my vices, my bad inclinations and passions, e.g., envy, love of food and drink? Have I been proud and boastful, thinking myself better in the sight of God and despising others as less important than myself? Have I imposed my own will on others, without respecting their freedom and rights?

2. What use have I made of time, of health and strength, of the gifts God has given me to be used like the talents in the Gospel? Do I use them to become more perfect every day? Or have I been lazy and too much given to leisure?

3. Have I been patient in accepting the sorrows and disappointments of life? How have I performed mortification so as to "fill up what is wanting to the sufferings of Christ"? Have I kept the precept of fasting and abstinence?

4. Have I kept my senses and my whole body pure and chaste as a temple of the Holy Spirit consecrated for resurrection and glory, and as a sign of God's faithful love for men and women, a sign that is seen most perfectly in the sacrament of matrimony? Have I dishonored my body by fornication, impurity, unworthy conversation or thoughts, evil desires, or actions? Have I given in to sensuality? Have I indulged in reading, conversation, shows, and entertainments that offend against Christian and human decency? Have I encouraged others to sin by my own failure to maintain these standards? Have I been faithful to the moral law in my married life?

5. Have I gone against my conscience out of fear or hypocrisy?

6. Have I always tried to act in the true freedom of the sons of God according to the law of the Spirit, or am I the slave of forces within me?